An Experimental Study of
The Effect of the Use of the Typewriter
on Beginning Reading

By

CECILIA E. UNZICKER, Ph.D.

Teachers College, Columbia University
Contributions to Education, No. 610

Published with the Approval of
Professor Arthur I. Gates, *Sponsor*

Bureau of Publications
Teachers College, Columbia University
NEW YORK CITY
1934

PRINTED IN
THE UNITED STATES OF AMERICA

THE RUMFORD PRESS
CONCORD, N. H.

ACKNOWLEDGMENTS

To Professor Arthur I. Gates, sponsor of the study, the writer is deeply grateful for invaluable help and encouragement throughout the investigation and during the preparation of the manuscript. To the other members of her committee, Professors James R. McGaughy and Rollo G. Reynolds, she wishes to express thanks and appreciation for their untiring aid and inspiration in the study. Gratitude is due Dr. Ralph Haefner for assistance in planning the study and for valued criticism of the manuscript; to the principals and teachers in the schools who so kindly gave their cooperation during the experiment; and to the members of the seminar in Elementary Education of Teachers College, who contributed valuable challenges.

It is the wish of the writer to acknowledge here the great debt she owes her mother, without whose help and encouragement the study would not have been completed.

C. E. U.

CONTENTS

CONTENTS

TABLES

CHARTS

CHAPTER I

REASONS FOR INVESTIGATION OF THE PROBLEM

THE proposal to introduce the typewriter as an instrument of instruction in the education of the very young child has recently come before parents, teachers, and school administrators in the form of a suggestion for serious and immediate consideration. Out of this suggestion the present study grew.

This does not mean, however, that the idea of a relationship between the typewriter and child education is new. In the December 16, 1875 issue of *The Nation* an advertisement proclaimed that no device is comparable to the typewriter for teaching children "to spell and punctuate." In the first typewriter catalogue ever published, which appeared in 1874, the value of the typewriter to children was emphasized. So the idea is as old as the machine itself. From 1890 to the present time statements by schoolmen and educators may be found expressing their belief that the typewriter is decidedly an asset in the classroom.

A. W. Bacheler [1] in June, 1899, wrote: "It is scarcely a decade since the introduction of the machine [typewriter] as a part of the outfit for regular school work attracted attention." He goes on to mention its introduction into high schools of Lynn and Gloucester, Massachusetts, as an original movement in 1890, and expresses his opinion that the age for starting typewriting is after handwriting has become somewhat fixed. His list of testimonials from other schoolmen of the time contains expressions in favor of the use of the typewriter in high schools as an aid in formal English work and in commercial preparation; but none of the men quoted advocates its use in the elementary school.

In June, 1895, Frank H. Kasson [2] urged the introduction of the typewriter in elementary and high schools on purely literary grounds. He, also, tried to prove his contention by means of testimonials.

[1] Bacheler, A. W., "The Typewriter in the Public Schools," *Education*, XIX: 626–633, 1899.
[2] Kasson, Frank H., "The Typewriter a Coming Necessity in Schools," *Education*, XV: 615–623, 1895.

Most of them were expressions in favor of the use of the typewriter in the high school. One person, however, must have tried its effect on a very young child, for he states: "Children almost babes will learn to copy even before they know their letters . . . ; this brings them to the knowledge of the actual significance and relation of the letters."

William A. Mowry [3] in June, 1891, expressed the wish that all work in English composition might be done with the printed form of letters instead of the script. He proposed having one typewriter in every classroom of fifty pupils. He was confidently looking forward to a time when school boards throughout the country would adopt the machine. Mowry's quotations are interesting and would be significant were it not that there is reason for questioning the validity of the methods of investigation. For example, he says: "Experiments made with some quite young children show that by the use of one of these instruments they will learn to read, spell and write in less time than they learn to do one of these things under the present method of instruction. . . ." The conditions of the experiment are not given, nor is the difference in length of time stated. Later occurs this rather extravagant statement: "A gentleman who traveled extensively among schools of New England recently said that everywhere the teachers who have tried the experiment of using the typewriter in school, pronounce unqualifiedly in its favor."

In June, 1892, Frank H. Palmer [4] prophesied that in five years more the use of the typewriter would be almost universal. He said that the schools must help and were helping: "The past six months [January to June, 1892] have witnessed a decided advance, both in the actual introduction of machines [typewriters] into the school-room and in the appreciation of their relations to education by leading educators." He forecast the general introduction and use of the typewriter in schools in "a comparatively few more years." He referred to its use in schools as having passed the experimental stage; and he listed six advantages growing out of its use as a purely educational instrument aside from its industrial value.

Frank Waldo [5] in 1902 prophesied that the typewriter would be-

[3] Mowry, William A., "The Educational Use of the Typewriter in Schools," *Education*, XI: 625–637, 1891.

[4] Palmer, Frank H., "Educational Aspects of Typewriting," *Education*, XII: 622–629, 1892.

[5] Waldo, Frank, "Educational Use of the Typewriter," *Education*, XXII: 484–492, 1902.

come a family necessity; but he believed that because of its bulkiness and costliness, it could never fully take the place of the pen or pencil.

In spite of all these utterances in favor of the typewriter as an educational instrument, few of them were in favor of its use in the elementary school. Where such use was advocated, no evidence was produced to show that conclusions were based upon scientific investigations. Experimentation, as these writers referred to it, meant experience with the machines in certain New England elementary schools and the collecting of subjective opinions of teachers. A few writers referred to good effects on grammar, reading, writing, and spelling; but again no scientific experimentation was done to verify these statements. Then, too, in that era, typewriters were bulky and costly compared with those available today. It is no wonder that school authorities and parents considered the results too difficult to obtain.

Today there is available an inexpensive portable typewriter which has been shown experimentally to have values when used by kindergarten and first grade children.[6] Since it requires only one muscular movement to write each letter on the typewriter compared with eight movements for some letters written by hand, it is the belief of many that the use of the typewriter may encourage the written expression of kindergarten and first grade children who are not developed enough to write script or manuscript easily.

As early as 1929, before the results of experimentation were recorded, Helen Thomas Follett[7] through thoughtful experience became convinced that no tool is so well adapted to encouragement of self-expression in language as the typewriter. She tells how the typewriter functioned in the education of her daughter, who began to use it at the age of four. During a ten-year period Mrs. Follett watched and directed the education of her daughter without help from a school. She gave written prose the most important place in her scheme of education. She believed that the child had something to say worth the trouble of written prose, but that pen and pencil were entirely useless as tools. She says, "Nor do I think that the pen is of any real use to a child as a practical tool; it is stiff,

[6] Haefner, Ralph, *The Typewriter in the Primary and Intermediate Grades* (The Macmillan Company, New York, 1932).
[7] Follett, Mrs. Helen Thomas, "Education via the Typewriter," *Parents*, VII: 22–24, 1932; "Education a la Carte," *Pictorial Review*, XXX: 2, 1929.

laborious, clumsy, and years are gone before it becomes flexible and manageable. Books have been written by parents, by teachers, and by psychologists about the imaginative life of the child from five to twelve years, but there has been scarcely a trace of that life recorded by the child himself. Isn't the pen the reason for this reticence?" Mrs. Follett recorded her child's progress during these ten years and kept all the written papers on file. It is interesting to note her comments on the child's progress in typewriting drill: "It is from the file itself that I gather the following items: that the child's use of the typewriter at four years old was jerky and halting; at five, slow but fairly accurate; at seven, competent and correct; and at eight it had become a tool entirely under her control, used without conscious effort. It [the record] shows, also, that just as gradually as the typewriting itself demanded less concentration, just so gradually did the child's thoughts find clearer and fuller expression."

Progressive educators throughout the country at the present time are concerned with the introduction of materials of instruction which will facilitate the development of satisfactory skills in the tool subjects, such as reading and writing. Without facility in the use of these fundamental subjects, it is difficult to achieve success either in or out of school. For this reason it seems essential for children to learn to use them at an early stage of their school careers. Then, when there is a question concerning the wisdom of introducing materials of instruction which seem conducive to any particular educational outcome, all of the concomitant effects of the use of the materials need to be considered. The question naturally arises whether the use of the materials will aid or hinder the development of any of these basic tool subjects, which are necessary in the present social order.

Thus it is that educators and reading specialists are concerned immediately with the effect on reading of the use of typewriters by young children. There are several reasons for this concern. In the first place, reading is considered the most important tool, since it is essential to human welfare and fundamental to the learning of nearly every other school subject. A hindrance to learning to read is more serious than a hindrance to learning to write or spell. An analysis of the conception of present-day American instruction in reading reveals another cause for concern if typewriters are introduced. We are living during a period of "emphasis upon broadened objectives in reading." [8] This is characterized by conceiving of reading as an educational experience rather than by interpreting it as a mechanical process or as a cultural or utilitarian asset, as was done in the past. This change of emphasis has caused methods of teaching reading to change. Instead of learning the alphabet first, learning to recognize isolated words next, learning next to read these elements in connected sentences, and finally putting sentences together to make connected meaning, quite the reverse order is followed. From the beginning, reading functions as a part of the educational life of the child. The greater emphasis is placed upon the thought of the reading content for the purpose of enriching, broadening, and varying his experiences. The pupil is directed to read meaningful material from the first; in other words, from the beginning he reads words, sentences, or paragraphs to get the thought instead of first directing attention to letter forms or phonograms. The development of the mechanics of reading, which is necessary in the process of learning to read, is accomplished most effectively by means of "a type of organization of a reading situation which guides or impels the pupil to react in a desired way while his efforts are directed to accurate interpretation and normal enjoyment of the content." [9] By this procedure practice in the particular skill desired is introduced in the actual reading process. Supplementary devices for recognizing letters and phonograms in isolation are then used only when the teacher is unable to invent a better intrinsic method for developing the needed reading mechanics.

With these accepted objectives in teaching reading and with a realization that the direct method is more productive of results, educators—first grade teachers especially—are alert to the difficulties which attend a first emphasis on letters and elements of words. For this reason some of them are asking the questions: Will the introduction of typewriters into homes, kindergartens, and first grades thwart our efforts to teach the child to read primarily for thought and enjoyment? Will it cause the pupil to become letter or word conscious? Will it lessen his eye span and slow up his reading? If it is introduced before reading has been started, will it impair his reading so that his initial progress will be retarded? Will he become a jerky word reader? A second group of teachers and schoolmen

[8] Smith, Nila B., "An Historical Analysis of American Reading Instruction." Unpublished Doctor's dissertation, Columbia University, June, 1931.
[9] Gates, Arthur I., *The Improvement of Reading*, p. 27.

with the same modern conception of reading is asking these questions: Will the use of the typewriter aid the child in learning to read? Will it aid him in the recognition of letters and words in such a way that his reading will be helped?   Will it help him to get ready for reading?   Will it help him realize a need for learning to read?   Will it help him to realize what the reading process means as a help in his daily experiences?   Will he learn to read more quickly if he uses the typewriter?   A third group is asking whether the use of typewriters has any effect on learning to read.   Has it any more effect on reading than has writing words, sentences, or paragraphs with pencil?

Thus there is a need for scientific research which can help us to decide just how the typewriter affects beginning reading if it affects it at all.   In the present investigation an attempt is made to answer certain of these questions (see page 28) through controlled experimentation and through careful interpretation of the findings.

CHAPTER II

HISTORICAL SURVEY OF METHODS OF TEACHING READING AND WRITING

Development of Methods of Teaching Reading

As was indicated in Chapter I, there is some theoretical ground for hesitating to introduce a child to the typewriter either before he is in the beginning stages of reading or immediately after. A brief history of reading instruction in America will indicate more clearly the reasons for such hesitancy.

Nila Banton Smith [1] has recently completed a study in which she traced and analyzed the successive developments in American reading instruction. Her findings are the result of historical and analytical research, made with the purpose of determining the successive periods of emphasis in American reading instruction and the influences which brought them about, and investigating the various developments within each of these periods. Miss Smith classifies the periods of emphasis under the following categories: [2] (1) Period of Religious Emphasis, 1620–1776; (2) Period of Patriotic-Moralistic Emphasis, 1776–1840; (3) Period of Emphasis upon German-Pestalozzian Principles, 1840–1880; (4) Period of Emphasis upon Reading as a Cultural Asset, 1880–1918; (5) Period of Emphasis upon Reading as a Utilitarian Asset, 1918–1925; (6) Period of Emphasis upon Broadened Objectives in Reading, 1925–.

PERIOD OF RELIGIOUS EMPHASIS

During the first period (Religious Emphasis, 1620–1776) [3] major effort in the teaching of reading was exerted to aid in saving the soul, and to that end much religious material was used. To give control over the mechanics of oral reading was the outstanding specific

---

[1] Smith, Nila B., "An Historical Analysis of American Reading Instruction." Unpublished Doctor's dissertation, Columbia University, June, 1931.

[2] *Ibid.*

[3] In the discussion that follows the interpretations and chronological divisions given by Miss Smith to the various periods of emphasis have been used.

objective. Spelling and reading were closely interdependent. Individual needs in reading were largely disregarded, or were not recognized.

The ABC method was a very popular method of instruction in reading. First the child learned the alphabet forward and backward, and occasionally he was encouraged to learn to recognize the individual letters in isolation. He spelled syllables and words, he memorized sections of content important in religious training, and he read orally; all this he did under teacher control. The unit of approach was letters. No phonetics was taught.

Words which would lend themselves to a logical organization of increasing syllables were selected for the primer vocabulary. *The New England Primer* introduced 391 words on the first ten pages, with a range of 7 to 69 new words per page. *Fox's Speller* introduced 320 words, with a range of 9 to 28. No provision was made for repetition of words. In only a few spellers were teaching instructions found; these stated rules for spelling and for observing "stops" and "points." The basic materials of instruction were the Hornbook, a primer written by a printer or a minister, a speller, and a copy of the Bible. No supplementary materials were used. Reading was selected which would instill in the minds of the young their duty toward God. Many Biblical quotations were included. The predominating subject matter, besides religious materials, was lists of syllables and words. The books were bound in board, paper, or leather covers from 4 x 4 inches to 3 x 6 inches in size. The paper was coarse, unglazed, and of a deep cream hue; and the type was fine and closely compressed.

PERIOD OF PATRIOTIC-MORALISTIC EMPHASIS

During the second period (Patriotic-Moralistic Emphasis, 1776–1840) the general aim in teaching reading was to prepare for the nationalistic-moralistic life of the adult. The specific aims were to give control over *expressive* oral reading and elocutionary delivery, to develop the mechanics of reading, and to purify American language. Reading and spelling were integrated closely, and it became important to include the subject matter of history and geography in the readers. Individual differences among children were disregarded because all must be fitted for the same nationalistic life.

The reading activities involved drill on the alphabet, drill in spelling, drill on sounds of letters, practice in expressive oral reading, memorization of rules for reading and speaking, and practice in the various phases of elocutionary delivery—all under teacher control as prescribed by the author of the textbook. The unit of approach was letters. Phonetics was introduced in the first reading lesson by sounding each letter forcefully and distinctly even though it was embedded in a syllable.

For primer vocabulary, words were selected which would lend themselves to a logical organization of increasing syllables. In Webster's *Speller* similarity of sounds determined the selection of words also. Webster's *American Spelling Book* introduced 487 words on the first ten pages, with a range of 25 to 197 new words per page; the *Franklin Primer* had 380 words on the first ten pages, with a range of 13 to 178 new words per page. No provision was made for repetition. Teaching instructions were in the form of definitely prescribed rules and notes placed in the textbook, mostly in regard to elocutionary delivery and pronunciation.

The basic materials used during this period were a speller or a primer plus one or two advanced readers; but there was no supplementary reading material. The predominating subject matter of the books included rules for enunciation and elocutionary delivery, lists of syllables and words of increasing length, nationalistic materials, and oratorical selections. The predominating types of literature were exposition, oration, dialogue, and poetry.

The mechanical make-up of books showed some improvement over that of the preceding period. The covers of the books were made of board or cardboard overlaid with blue or tan paper, and they varied in size from 3 x 4½ inches to 4 x 6½ inches. The paper was usually coarse, and deep cream in color. The type was fine, closely compressed, but clearer and better spaced than in the previous period. The authors of the textbooks were usually schoolmasters holding the degree of Bachelor of Arts or Master of Arts and having teaching experience in the elementary grades.

PERIOD OF EMPHASIS ON GERMAN-PESTALOZZIAN PRINCIPLES

The third period (Emphasis upon German-Pestalozzian Principles, 1840–1880) is also referred to as the period of the alphabet-phonetic method. The major aim was to equip the masses with the reading skill and knowledge necessary for intelligent citizenship. Two of the more specific aims were identical with those of the preceding period: to gain control over *expressive* oral reading and elocutionary delivery, and to purify American language. Another specific objective was added: to give information on different subjects. Reading and spelling were closely integrated; also, writing came into wider use as a help in teaching beginning reading. No attention was given to individual differences, for all were to conform to the same methods and materials in order to gain the skill necessary for adult reading.

The activities engaged in included drill on naming and sounding letters and spelling words, practice in expressive oral reading, practice in the various phases of elocutionary delivery, defining words and noting errors of pronunciation, and answering questions based on the text. The unit of approach was still the letters of the alphabet. Phonetics was introduced in the first lesson. It was taught by sounding each letter separately and also by noting similarities of certain combinations of letters.

For the primer vocabulary words were selected which lent themselves to repetition and phonetic analysis and which represented objects and experiences familiar to children. The *McGuffey First Reader* introduced 305 words on the first ten pages, with a range of 10 to 12. *Tower's Primer* had 297 on the first ten pages, with a range of 3 to 10. Direct provision was usually made for repeating new words on several pages. Teaching instructions appeared in the textbook; they were definitely prescribed rules and notes in regard to spelling, phonetics, elocutionary delivery, pronunciation, and sometimes content. The basic materials were a graded series of readers, including a reader for each of the first six grades. The primers contained realistic materials, whereas the advanced readers had a wide range covering morals, economics, politics, literature, history, science, and philosophy. The primers were made up of unrelated sentences; the advanced readers held realistic narration, exposition, and poetry.

The readers were bound with cardboard covers, overlaid with paper or leather, varying from 3 x 4½ inches to 4 x 6½ inches. The paper was unglazed, light cream in color, with rough edges, and of finer texture than that used previously. The type in first readers was approximately the same as that in present readers; lines were broken miscellaneously, and script sentences appeared frequently. There was an improvement in the artistic quality of the books, for the lithographic reproductions were superior to those in previous readers. These pictures represented animals, objects, or simple human relationships within children's experiences, and occupied from 5 per cent to 20 per cent of the total number of pages in primers. The books were written usually by college professors (men) having the degree of Bachelor of Arts or Master of Arts, with or without teaching experience in the elementary grades.

PERIOD OF EMPHASIS UPON READING AS A CULTURAL ASSET

During the fourth period (Emphasis upon Reading as a Cultural Asset, 1880–1918) the general purpose in teaching reading was to contribute to adult culture by developing appreciation of good literature and permanent interest in it.   During this period the objective of elocutionary delivery lost its strong hold, and three new specific objectives were added: to develop literary appreciation, to develop a permanent interest in reading, to develop a thoughtful attitude toward meanings.   Frequent attempts were made to correlate language and nature work with reading.   It was during this period that authors first came to recognize the interests of little children.   Such recognition took the form of reading devices, colored pictures, stories with a plot.   There was little adjustment to individual needs, however.   All were to conform to a prescribed method because that was supposed to be the best way to achieve the reading objectives.

Activities connected with reading included dramatizing and memorizing stories from literature, using letter cards for seat work, phonetic drill and word drill, practice in expressive oral reading but without elocutionary artificiality, and answering thought questions based on the text.   The method of approach was to tell the story and dramatize it, then read the sentences, later breaking them into phrases and words and eventually applying phonetics.   Thus the sentence was the unit of approach.   The time for introducing phonics was after the vocabulary of the first story had been learned. The new word was analyzed into consonant and phonogram; elements were blended to make the word; and the initial consonant was then changed to make a new word.

Words necessary in telling an interesting story from literature were selected for primer vocabulary.   The *Reading-Literature Primer* introduced 31 new words in the first ten pages, with a range of 0 to 6 new words per page; the *Story-Hour Primer* had 72 new words in the first ten pages, with a range of 0 to 19.   There was more repetition of vocabulary than ever before; it occurred naturally in cumulative tales containing a series of episodes, in which only one simple new incident was added at a time. A definite procedure was prescribed in the teacher's manual for teaching by the sentence method, and there was very little leeway allowed for teacher initiative. The basic reading materials consisted of a graded series, including a primer and six readers; the supplementary materials were flash cards covering words and phonetic elements, charts containing lists of phonetic families, and letter cards for seat work. The content in the primers was a medium for oral reading practice with the aim of stimulating children's interest in reading and developing a taste for good literature. Mother Goose stories and folk and fairy tales were used largely.

The mechanical make-up of the books showed further improvement. Covers were made of gray or tan cloth and decorated with a picture in one or two colors. The pages were much larger, varying in size from 5¾ x 7½ inches to 6⅜ x 7¾ inches. The paper was smooth, unglazed, light cream in color, and sufficiently heavy so that print would not show through. The type was of uniform size throughout each book, with wider spacing than that used before in primers. The sentences in the primer and first reader were divided between phrases, and vocabulary lists in back of books were included. From 31 per cent to 34 per cent of the space was used for illustrations. Scenes and characters from folk and fairy tales predominated in the pictures. Children as well as animals were drawn; the figures were large and much action was shown; the general effects were artistic but somewhat cluttered with detail. The authors generally were either two women, principal and teacher, or a man superintendent and a woman supervisor, all having elementary experience and normal school training.

PERIOD OF EMPHASIS UPON READING AS A UTILITARIAN ASSET

During the fifth period (Emphasis upon Reading as a Utilitarian Asset, 1918–1925) the general purpose in teaching reading was to prepare for the efficient use of reading ability in the practical affairs of life. More specifically, the objective of developing expressive oral reading met with a decline, and the development of literary appreciation received much less attention; the new objective was to develop skill in rapid comprehensive silent reading. Basal readers were making rather general provision in primary grades for direct correlation of reading with other subjects, such as handwork, language, number work, and rhythm, to be subservient to the reading exercise. Reading was still taught as a separate subject. In this period of utilitarian emphasis the wide use of reading tests and the appearance of much literature on diagnostic and remedial work directed attention to individual needs. Ability grouping of reading classes on the basis of degree of intelligence was recommended for the first time.

The activities engaged in were practice in exercises to increase comprehension and speed in silent reading, phrase and word drill with phonetic drill usually; seat work calling for following directions and matching question-answer exercises; and some oral reading. The method of approach was usually reading directions silently and responding with dramatizations, drawings, or construction work; and the unit of approach was largely sentences or a combination of sentences, words, and phrases. Ear training was usually given in connection with the first lessons; formal phonics began at the end of four or five weeks. Phonetics was introduced by oral exaggeration of like sounds in rhymes and jingles; later the children sounded separate letters, diphthongs, and families consisting of vowels attached to their succeeding consonants.

There was a pronounced tendency to reduce the size of primer vocabularies; usually words which would be familiar to children were selected. The *Bolenius Primer* introduced 39 new words on the first ten pages, with a range of 0 to 8 new words per page; the *Winston Primer*, 34 new words, with a range of 0 to 7. Repetition was provided for largely by reinforcing the reading vocabulary with silent reading exercises, seat work, and games. Teaching instructions gave definitely prescribed procedure emphasizing silent reading; some leeway, however, was provided for teacher initiative. Some teachers' manuals contained discussions of investigations and suggestions for seat work. At this time the number of basal readers increased to eight readers and a primer. The period of utilitarian emphasis brought with it elaborate sets of flash cards to increase eye span, silent reading seat work materials, and diagnostic and remedial tests. Emphasis was placed on selection of content which would appeal to children's interests and also lend itself to different types of silent reading exercises. The predominating subject matter contained realistic stories, informational selections, and silent reading exercises in the form of narrative and expository materials and poems.

The books became more attractive in their mechanical make-up;

the paper was better in quality, and the type was large and clear. Sentences in primers and first readers were divided between phrases. From 28 per cent to 32 per cent of the space was given to illustrations; these were both realistic and fantastic. The authorship of these books swung back to people with college degrees—frequently women in public school positions or men college professors working separately and not in collaboration.

PERIOD OF EMPHASIS UPON BROADENED OBJECTIVES IN READING

In the sixth period (Emphasis upon Broadened Objectives, 1925–) the teaching of reading has as its general purposes (1) preparing for the efficient utilization of reading in the practical affairs of life and (2) developing appreciation of its recreational aspects as they contribute to well-rounded living. The specific objectives become broad and varied: to develop strong motives for reading and permanent interest in it; to extend experience; to stimulate thought; to improve reading tastes; to develop skill in the several different types of ability required in both the silent and the oral reading of work-type and recreatory materials. Basal readers are making rather general provision in primary grades for direct correlation of reading with other subjects. The highest degree of integration thus far is found in the type of instruction provided by teachers who allow no systematized set of readers, but teach reading largely as it enters into, or grows out of, children's activities and interests. At the present time ability grouping is advocated, not on the sole basis of intelligence, but also in consideration of such factors as these: reading ability or abilities, social background, emotional maturity, reading interests.

In the method advocated by present readers children do both oral and silent reading of work-type and recreatory materials supplemented with various kinds of practices designed to develop different reading abilities. Some schools not using a particular system of readers let reading largely grow out of, and feed into, the children's own activities and interests, with some special provision for groups or individuals in need of particular kinds of practice. Activities involved are: (1) excursions or experiences (social, scientific, industrial, creative) with reading as an outgrowth; (2) composing charts, booklets, and newspapers; (3) some practice in various reading books to develop skill; (4) some drill in word recognition and phonics, often incidental; (5) reading in search of information to use in various activities; (6) reading literature in connection with creative work, also for aesthetic pleasure. The unit of approach is a small but entire unit of thought, later analyzed into sentences, phrases, and words. Some teachers are using children's own compositions which constitute a complete but short unit of thought. Phonetics is taught more moderately at the present time than previously; and the time for introducing it is the stage when the child begins to notice likenesses and differences in words—usually at the end of ten weeks of reading experience. Some incidental reference is made to phonics in general lessons; and groups of individuals who are in need of phonetic practice are given special exercises. The methods and values of teaching phonetics are being questioned. Previous reference has been made to Gates's findings on the values of teaching phonetics intrinsically. As a result of these findings, much workbook reading material constructed for this purpose is in use, and supplementary materials for phonetic purposes are used only when better means are not available.

Authors of readers at the present time base their vocabulary selection upon words having the highest frequency in scientifically determined word lists. There is an increasing tendency to reduce the size of vocabularies and the rate of introduction of new words. Repetition occurs in connection with common words which are needed repeatedly in the children's compositions. No teaching instructions are prescribed, and teaching procedure is left entirely to the teacher. There is a new trend toward separate courses of study for different phases of reading instruction or for the development of specific reading abilities. At the present time professional books concerning reading deal with a wide variety of subjects; children's interests, methods of teaching, and the psychology of learning are most frequently treated. Teachers' manuals offer some optional choices, although procedure by lessons is still generally prescribed.

Although the prediction is made by many educators that the basal series eventually will disappear, at the present time the majority of series contain three readers and a primer. Materials composed by the children and the teacher as an outgrowth of group and individual experiences and interests are used—also a wide variety of books which contribute to these experiences and interests and provide practice in reading. The present supplemental books are wide in variety, including realistic stories, informational materials, and modern fanciful tales. Little is being done to perpetuate old folklore. A new trend is seen in the publication of sets of small books, all of the same general nature, but each written on a different topic. The present period has popularized the "workpad" for silent reading seat work. The trend is toward a wider utilization of seat work periods as a time of creative and constructive activities, or as an opportunity to pursue individual interests in reading. Informal silent reading materials and flash cards to meet the various needs of class and individuals are prepared by teachers. The reading materials are so selected that they may contribute to the daily interests and enterprises of the class and provide practice in *all* grades. The predominating subject matter is social studies and science; the predominating types of literature are realistic stories, old tales from literature, modern fanciful tales, informational selections, and poems.

The books of this present period show improvement in their mechanical make-up, being fashioned more in accord with children's interests, practical utility, artistic qualities, and the physiological effects. Authorship of these readers is usually a joint undertaking by one or more women in public school work having the degree of Bachelor of Arts or Master of Arts, together with a professor holding the degree of Doctor of Philosophy.

From this history of reading instruction over the six periods traced and analyzed by Miss Smith certain developments may be noted that eventually led to reasons for investigating the effects of the use of the typewritter by first grade children on their beginning reading:

1. The change in objectives has made more and varied demands upon reading instruction, calling for scientific introspection in regard to methods and results.

2. Reading cannot be thought of as a subject apart from any other. Therefore, if typewriting is viewed basically as an instrument of expression or as a language tool, the effects of typewriting upon reading should be weighed.

3. The change in the unit of approach from letters of the alphabet to children's own compositions which constitute a complete but short unit of thought raises a real issue concerning the use of typewriters: Will their use give undue emphasis to letters and so distract from the unit of thought, which should be given first emphasis?

4. The result of scientific experimentation,[4] which shows insufficient transfer of training so that certain words and elements of themselves may be known but may not be recognized in a reading situation, raises the question whether this result may be applicable to experiences with letters and words on the typewriter. In other words, owing to the lack of transfer of training, may experiences with letters and words on the typewriter have practically no effect on learning to read?

5. A growing recognition of individual differences in learning and of the complexity of the reading process attaches importance to investigating the effects of typewriting to find out whether all children are affected in the same way. It should also be known whether abilities in reading are aided or hindered in their development by the use of the typewriter; and if so, which abilities are aided and which are hindered.

6. The selection of a limited vocabulary, the rate of introduction of new words and the amount of repetition of words in readers, the use of professional books and manuals by teachers, the improved mechanical make-up of books, the broad range of subject matter, the authorship of books by people thoroughly prepared in the profession—the development of each of these is an indication of a trend in the direction of dignifying the teaching of reading as a science worthy of thorough study.

DEVELOPMENT OF METHODS OF TEACHING WRITING

M. L. Dougherty, in her article, "History of the Teaching of Handwriting in America," [5] divides the teaching of handwriting in America into five periods: Colonial Period, 1600–1800; Transition Period, 1800–1850; Period of Independent Elaboration of American Systems, 1850–1890; Vertical-Writing Movement, 1890–1900; Combination of Commercial and Scientific Influences, 1900–1916.

COLONIAL PERIOD, 1600–1800

During the Colonial Period certain schools were devoted solely to teaching writing, since the skill of penmanship was highly esteemed. Only crude materials were available, such as the quill

---

[4] Gates, Arthur I., "The Supplementary Device versus the Intrinsic Method of Teaching Reading," *Elementary School Journal*, XXVI: 775–786, 1925.

[5] Dougherty, M. L., "History of the Teaching of Handwriting in America," *Elementary School Journal*, XVIII: 280–286, 1917.

pen, rough paper, birch-bark (a paper substitute), and homemade ink. The instructor was called upon to make the pens and keep them in repair and to set up individual copies. Later, with the invention of lithography, the master was relieved of "copy-setting" and could give more attention to the actual teaching.

TRANSITION PERIOD, 1800–1850

After the Revolution the nationalistic views of the people led to the attempt to provide American texts and materials for schools. At this time writing-books with ruled lines came into use, but they were without copies and samples of good penmanship. Quill pens and plummets gave way to steel pens and lead pencils. With this introduction of new materials, the instructor was freer to give attention to teaching penmanship.

The method of teaching, the style of writing, the position of hand and arm, and the kind of writing desks used were the fundamental factors considered in the teaching of writing during this period. Pestalozzi's theories were adopted, which involved the measuring of height of letters and the spacing of letters by horizontal and vertical lines. The elementary strokes were taught first, and were identified by number so that the teacher did not dictate a letter but pronounced each element in succession. Another method, which originated in England during this period, was introduced into this country by B. F. Foster. This was muscular-movement writing, which placed importance upon the manner of writing rather than upon its form. The children wore elaborate arrangements of straps to hold their fingers in correct position while forms of letters were explained and exercises were given.

PERIOD OF INDEPENDENT ELABORATION OF
AMERICAN SYSTEMS, 1850–1890

During the period 1850–1890 the methods were to teach the elementary movements first and then combine these into more complex movements. The theory sponsored by Foster accented the arm movement. Letter forms of distinct type, and graded book series appeared. The demand for efficient writing led to the introduction of special writing classes in commercial schools. These schools installed courses for teaching writing in elementary schools; but since the authors had no experience with child problems, they failed to adapt the work to the elementary stage of development.

Between 1890 and 1900 vertical writing was introduced in an effort to remedy faults of posture and eye strain. But this style was soon abandoned, because it proved inefficient in producing speed and legibility. From the vertical-writing movement, however, there resulted a less extreme slant than that used previously.

COMBINATION OF COMMERCIAL AND SCIENTIFIC INFLUENCES, 1900–1916

A demand for speed and form was made during the first two decades of the twentieth century. Commercial schools adopted movement exercises and the use of rhythm by counting for drill methods. These methods influenced somewhat the teaching of writing in public schools. Practice pads and "copy-slips" were used in addition to the old-style copy-book which was seldom used at that time. The demand for speed necessitated simplification of letter forms and elimination of non-essentials. Some of the systems carried this practice to an extreme, and the picturesque handwriting of the previous periods was lost. The problem of training teachers for teaching handwriting became prominent as more definite training came to be required. Many school systems required their teachers to secure a certificate in penmanship from one of the correspondence schools provided by makers of handwriting systems.

CURRENT PERIOD, 1916–

During the present period the methods of teaching penmanship are quite different from the methods of the former periods. "The modern goals in penmanship teaching differ from the traditional in that pupils now write, not for the sake of imitating a set model, but for the sake of conveying ideas. The first step is to stimulate the child to a purpose in writing—a desire to write a letter or fill out a bank slip. The second step is so to equip him with methods of work that he will attack his writing problems intelligently." [6] This modern conception of writing has caused changes in the teaching of writing to primary school children. Manuscript as a form of writing has been substituted for script in many schools because of its adaptability to the needs and aptitudes of young children. At the present time it is contended by some educators that the

[6] Alltucker, M. M., "Teaching of Handwriting," *National Education Association Journal*, XVI: 25, 1927.

practice of typewriting by kindergarten and first grade pupils will encourage self-expression in written language.

History of Writing [7]

The history of writing involves the whole history of civilization, from the earliest stages of savagery to the present status of comparative enlightenment and efficiency.

There are three distinct stages in the growth of writing, although they are not hard and fast chronological stages: (1) the stage representing such devices as the knotted handkerchief, the notched stick, or the Peruvian quipus used to assist memory and to record passing events; (2) the stage of picture writing or ideographs used extensively by the Assyrians, the Egyptians, and the Chinese; and (3) the transitional stage of development from ideographs to syllabaries and alphabets.

Changes in materials and implements used for the inscriptions have been at work ever since any kind of writing started.   Following the crudest materials, such as clay, sticks, stones, and birch-bark, we find relics of very early writing implements and materials used by the Egyptians: reed pens either frayed out or cut to a point at one end, papyrus, black ink made of lamp black, and red ink made of iron oxide.   Vellum, parchment, and wax tablets are mentioned as later writing materials.   In the middle of the fifteenth century Johann Gutenburg's printing press appeared as the first mechanical writing instrument.   Since then printing presses have been greatly improved.   A later mechanical writing machine, which is growing in its influence and may affect writing in the future, is the typewriter. The story of its development is of interest here.

History of the Typewriter [8]

James H. Collins [9] tells the story of how Father Sholes one July day in 1867 called his friends into his shop to see a "writing machine"

[7] The discussion in this section is based on the following references:
Lipman, Michael, *A History of the Alphabet* (Royal Typewriting Company. Bureau of Research, 1930).
Encyclopedia Britannica: Alphabet, I: 677–684, 1929; Palaeography, XVII: 96–102, 1929; Pictography, XVII: 913–914, 1929.
[8] Much of the discussion in this section is based on a monograph entitled *The Story of the Typewriter*, which was published in 1923 by the Herkimer County Historical Society of Herkimer, New York, as part of the celebration of the fiftieth anniversary of the typewriter.   (The real author's name is omitted.)
[9] Collins, James H., "The Story of the Typewriter," *St. Nicholas*, XLIX: 486–495, 1922.   Quotations on this and the following page are from this author.

—a device of his own invention made with some pieces of board, an old telegraph key, a sheet of glass, and other odds and ends: "Moving the paper slowly with one hand, he tapped the telegraph key with the other. On the end of the telegraph key was a letter 'w' cut in brass." One letter was written over and over like this: wwwwwwww www. But he saw that with thirty or forty such keys, each having a letter or a figure, he could make a machine that would write anything.

This was not, however, the first conception of the typewriter. In 1714 an Englishman, Henry Mill, took out a patent for a machine which was said to "impress letters on paper as in writing." "We know nothing more about it, however; nor about an 'embossing machine' invented in France in 1784; nor of the first American attempt at a writing-machine, called a 'typographer,' patented by a Mr. William A. Burt, all records of which were destroyed in a great fire in Washington in 1836."

The principle of the typebars as it is found in typewriters today was used by a Frenchman named Progin who patented a "typographic machine or pen." A typewriter capable of actual work was built in 1843 by an American named Charles Thurber. It had the carriage that holds the paper and slides along as a line is written, and a means of turning the paper when a line is finished.

Many instances could be given of how prominently the needs of the blind figured in the efforts of early inventors. For example, Pierre Foucault, a blind teacher in the Paris Institution for the Blind, invented a machine which successfully printed embossed letters for the blind. This machine was patented in France in 1849.

Oliver T. Eddy of Baltimore took out a patent for the next machine in 1850. It was patterned to furnish the means of substituting printed letters and signs for written ones in the transaction of business. The objection to it was that it was too cumbersome and intricate for practical use.

During the fifties there were numerous attempts at typewriter invention. J. M. Jones's machine in 1852 marked some progress. A. Ely Beach produced a machine in 1856 which was built to benefit the blind; it did good work but was slow in operation. Dr. Samuel W. Francis, a physician living in New York, received a patent for a machine in 1857; the keys resembled those of a piano and the types, which were circular in arrangement, printed at a common center. It was the first machine to print with speed exceeding that of a pen; but the objection was that it was too bulky and costly. There were a great many other attempts at producing a practical typewriter between 1854 and 1867; but, although they did good work, none could write with the speed necessary to justify its introduction into actual service. The need for such a machine was evident, and the solution of the problem came in the year 1867. Although its production was not to be initiated until seven years later in the little town of Ilion, New York, the construction of a practical appliance for writing purposes was begun in the outskirts of the city of Milwaukee in the winter of 1866–1867. In a small workshop three men started work on a writing device. They were Carlos Glidden, whose energies to that date had been expended for the purpose of improving farm machinery, and Samuel W. Soule and Christopher L. Sholes, both printers by trade. They knew of no prior efforts which would aid them except those of the Englishman, Pratt, whose "Pterotype" was described in the *Scientific American*. None of the three was a mechanic and so the services of one Matthias Schwalbach, an employee in the shop, were enlisted; and he contributed much to the development of the machine. After months of work the first machine was finished in the fall of 1867, and a patent for it was obtained the following June. The instrument was crude and odd in appearance, hardly recognizable today as a typewriter; but in spite of its many defects, it wrote rapidly and accurately. To try out their machine, the three inventors typed letters on it to their friends, among them James Densmore of Meadville, Pennsylvania. Densmore became so enthusiastic that he bought an interest in the invention by paying all the expenses already incurred. He became the business manager of the concern, a responsibility which the other members were incapable of assuming. Sholes' inventive genius led to the construction of the machine, while Densmore's faith and business energy carried it through to its salvation.

Early and numerous defects of the *typewriter*, so named by Sholes, were corrected by the suggestions of friends who were trying it out in practical situations and by the constant and tedious construction of new models, numbering from twenty-five to thirty before 1873. By this time the machine had been so perfected that it was presented to the Remington Gun-Making Company, whose further contributions to its development warranted its commercial manufacture. The first Remington machine resembled the sewing machine in appearance.   It was fitted to a stand with grape-vine pedestals, and a foot treadle was used to operate the carriage return.   It had no shift-key mechanism and wrote upper-case letters only.   The metal covering of the typewriter was similar to that of the sewing machine.   The efficient writing machines of today, although greatly improved since 1873, still show the same fundamental principles of construction embodied in this first typewriter.

One thing commonly lost sight of in the history of the development of the typewriter is that there was really no suitable typewriter available to children until the latter part of 1920.   That was the year in which the first strictly portable typewriter was brought out with a standard, four-row keyboard.   Portables with four-row key-boards were not produced by all the four leading manufacturers, however, until about 1925.   Previously, all the small typewriters even moderately suited to children had had only three rows of type-keys, and two shifts.   Such a typewriter called for too much manual skill to be well adapted to the average child.   It is difficult to persuade even professional typists to use typewriters equipped with only three rows of keys.

CHAPTER III

EXPERIMENTAL BACKGROUND FOR USING TYPEWRITERS IN FIRST GRADE

UP to the time of the present study very little scientific data have been available from which one could determine whether typewriting has any effect whatever on beginning reading.

The results of an experimental study made by Ben D. Wood and Frank N. Freeman, which involved the use of typewriters in the classrooms of fifty-odd elementary schools in twelve cities throughout the United States, appeared in 1932.[1] The study had been carried on over a period of three years, with several hundred teachers and a total of 14,949 pupils of the kindergarten and first six grades participating.

The object of this research was to secure sufficient experimental evidence to prove that typewriters should or should not be adopted for regular use by children in the elementary school classroom. This study was concerned with the question of general fundamental educational significance, since the typewriter, if adopted, would be closely related to the subjects of the curriculum. The problem was to study the effect of typewriting as a supplement to handwriting rather than to study typewriting as a substitute for handwriting.

During the first year of the experiment the classes having typewriters, with a total of 6,125 pupils, were comparable to the control classes, with a total of 8,824 pupils, save that the latter had no typewriters. Care was taken to measure such factors of difference between groups as might be supposed to influence the results. Teachers were rated on the following items: amount of training, preparation for teaching, length of experience, local tenure, and rating by supervisors or other superiors. In all but the supervisors' ratings the teachers were essentially alike. The supervisors' ratings indicated that the experimental teachers were slightly superior. The curriculums of the two groups, which were drawn from the

[1] Wood, Ben D. and Freeman, Frank N., *An Experimental Study of the Educational Influences of the Typewriter in the Elementary Classroom* (*The Macmillan Company, New York, 1932*).

same cities, were substantially the same. The characteristics of the pupils were balanced so far as social and racial backgrounds were concerned; these two factors were considered when one class was equated with another. The groups were essentially the same in chronological age, and in intelligence as measured by the Pintner-Cunningham test for grades one and two and by the National Intelligence test for grades three to six inclusive. By means of the Gates Silent Reading Tests and the Stanford Achievement Test equality in initial achievement was obtained.

In order to measure educational influences the following achievement tests were given at both the beginning and the end of the school session: (*a*) complete Gates Reading Tests, or Stanford Achievement Test; (*b*) handwriting quality; (*c*) handwriting speed; (*d*) typewriting speed (only to experimental classes); (*e*) special spelling tests; and (*f*) certain other special tests. Also, a complete file of the written work for each experimental and control child was kept, for the purpose of comparing quality of written work.

Although the first year of experimental procedure involved both experimental and control groups, the second year's research supplemented the work already done by continuing experimentation with the experimental group. Progress of children made during the second year was compared with progress made during the first year. The experimental groups during the two years were approximately the same in number, but about one-third of them in the second year group had not taken part in the first year experiment.[2]

During the two years of the study the experimental groups used typewriters. Exactly the same type of educational treatment, except that the control pupils did not use the machines, was given to both groups.

In their study, Wood and Freeman found strong evidence to support the following conclusions: [3]

1. That it is feasible to use the typewriter in the conduct of the ordinary work in the elementary school.
2. That the average typing speed in the course of a year is approximately equal to the average handwriting rate and a considerable degree of typing accuracy is acquired.
3. That the use of the typewriter, as used in this experiment, does

[2] Freeman, F. N., "Experiment in the Use of Typewriters in the Elementary School," *Elementary School Journal*, XXXII: 752–759, 1932.
[3] Wood and Freeman, *op. cit.*, p. 184.

not result in any appreciable loss in handwriting quality or handwriting rate.

4. That the use of the typewriter tends to stimulate elementary school pupils to produce more written material than they would produce otherwise.

5. That it probably raises the level of achievement in certain school subjects, without any apparent loss in any subject.

6. That the teachers regard the typewriter as a valuable educational instrument and pupils look upon it with marked favor.

While the major purpose in this experiment was to find the general educational significance of the use of typewriters in the kindergarten and in the elementary school, the effect on beginning reading was noted in a general way. The set-up and procedure of the experiment have been explained. The results obtained at the end of the first year in grade one need to be taken into consideration here so that we may understand what has been discovered. In grade one, having 421 cases in the experimental group and 535 cases in the control group, it was found at the end of the first year that the experimental excess gain in Gates Type 1 test (word recognition) of .86 in raw score was 1.62 times its probable error of .53. In Gates Type 2 test (word, phrase, and sentence reading) the experimental excess gain of 2.91 in raw score or 0.15 in grade score was six times its probable error of .44. In Gates Type 3 test (paragraph meaning) the experimental excess gain of .41 in raw score or 0.10 in grade score was about 1.5 times its probable error of .26.[4] In the three phases of reading the differences in favor of the pupils who had used the typewriter were significantly larger than their probable errors. During the second year of the experiment it seems apparent that the gains of the experimental group over those of the control group are smaller than their first year gains;[5] but in view of uncertainties involved in the second year test data, these differences must be considered cautiously and reasonable allowances should be made. On the whole, however, Wood and Freeman feel that it seems safe to conclude that the second-year test data are in harmony with those of the first year in indicating superiority of experimental over control gains.

The second volume, a result of the study discussed above, assembles, organizes, and interprets in terms of practical school situations

[4] Wood and Freeman, *op. cit.*, p. 29.
[5] *Ibid.*, pp. 48–49.

the experience of the group of teachers who used the typewriters during the two-year experiment. It selects especially the data which throw light on urgent classroom problems. In regard to the typewriter and reading activities [6] in kindergarten and first grade, Haefner says, "The part which may be played by the typewriter in arousing reading interest is probably an important one. For example, many kindergarten children after copying a word on the machine are very eager to know what it 'says.' Others who have learned to type a few words ask the meaning of the phrases seen on posters, pictures, and labels. First grade children who have experienced the thrill of writing a few words frequently begin searching through magazines for interesting material to copy." [7] He shows examples of kindergarten papers to indicate that these young children are learning to write meaningful combinations of letters into word groups and thus are developing a grasp of word unity. "Gradually," he says, "the kindergarten child learns how to interpret or read a certain number of words which he writes. He can commonly identify his name after he has written it, as well as a few nouns, such as, *dog, cat,* and *boy.*" [8] Haefner points out in a paper written by a first grade pupil, who had used the machine for two months, that the child had observed the following mechanical phases of printed material: capitals at the beginning of a sentence, some punctuation mark at the end of a sentence, spacing between words, spacing between lines, and spelling. From this example he observes: "Recognition of these various mechanical elements has a bearing on interpretation of material. It does not seem too much to say, therefore, that for the first grade child his copying contributes to his reading." [9]

[6] Haefner, Ralph, *The Typewriter in the Primary and Intermediate Grades,* pp. 123–128.

[7] *Ibid.,* p. 124. [8] *Ibid.,* p. 125. [9] *Ibid.,* p. 128.

CHAPTER IV

DESCRIPTION OF THE INVESTIGATION

In the present investigation the problem of the effect of typewriting on beginning reading narrows itself to mean: What are the effects of the use of the typewriter on learning to read by first grade pupils when typewriting becomes an activity in the school program causing a subtraction of approximate proportioned amounts of each existing activity, equivalent to the time used for typewriting?

How do these effects compare with the effects on reading in existing first grade programs?

1. How does the use of the typewriter affect reading for thought?

   a. How does it affect ability to read and comprehend complete paragraphs?
   b. How does it affect word, phrase, and sentence reading; ability to read verbal units of increasing complexity?
   c. How does it affect word recognition; ability to read words representative of the primary vocabulary?

2. How does it affect oral reading habits and phonetic and other analytic skills in the actual process of reading?

3. How does it affect methods of studying and recognizing words?

   a. How does it affect word pronunciation and methods of attacking words?
   b. How does it affect ability to recognize and deal in certain ways with individual word elements?

4. How does it affect speed in reading?

5. How does it affect the visual perception of the reader; ability to note similarities and dissimilarities of words?

6. How does it affect an interest in reading?

   a. How many children choose to read during the "free period"?
   b. How many books does each child read during the year?

7. How does it affect general reading ability and detailed characteristics of reading as rated by the classroom teacher?

The problem now is not whether typewriters should or should not be included as part of the materials of instruction in the first or any other grade of the elementary school. Such a problem would call for research disclosing general effects upon a number of factors, together with effect upon reading in the first grade; this kind of experimentation has already been done in the Wood-Freeman study. Nor does the problem include effects of typewriting on reading in every kind of first grade and under all circumstances; there may be peculiarities in a certain first grade class which would make it so different from those used in this experiment that the same results could not be expected. It is not a problem of typewriting versus handwriting in script or manuscript, with the subsequent reading results of each. Also, the present problem does not contain the problem of an accepted method for teaching typewriting. The only problem of the present study is: How does typewriting, carried on as it has been in this research, affect the beginning reading of first grade children, like those described and in similar environment.

Reasons for the Experimental Set-Up Chosen

The "equivalent-groups" method of experimentation was used throughout. One group, known as the Experimental or Typewriter group, included those first grade children who spent from 75 to 90 minutes per week at the typewriter and during the rest of the school time engaged in the regular program of activities of their grade. The other group, known as the Control group, carried on the normal program of activities which ordinarily would have been pursued if the experiment had not been in progress. The groups were equated within classrooms so that each separate class had within it an Experimental and a Control group. Thus the Experimental and Control groups were not working as separate units except during periods when the Experimental group was typing; during this time the Control group was engaging in the activities of the ordinary school program, and a variety of things were done.

It was necessary to choose the equivalent-groups method of experimentation in this study, because a control experimental factor could not be dispensed with. Since learning to read in the first grade is integrated with, and affected directly by, all elements in the first grade environment, it is readily seen that the total net change in the trait or traits in question in this experiment produced by irrelevant factors—disturbing factors of considerable magnitude— is unavoidable. Compared to the influence of the experimental factor, typewriting, most of these irrelevant factors exercise a comparatively large influence.   In conferences with the present writer, a number of primary reading specialists expressed the belief that the first grade teacher herself is one of the most influential factors on the beginning reading of her pupils; that is, regardless of similarity in training, in years of experience, in supervisors' ratings, and in courses of study followed, no two teachers in the first grade affect beginning reading in the same way.   Therefore this multitude of possible influences on reading, other than typewriting, had to be controlled by creating a group as equivalent as possible to the Experimental group, with the same teacher and the same total school situation and social environment.   From each classroom was drawn an equal number of both Experimental and Control children, and an attempt was made to equate as many children as possible within separate classrooms in order to strengthen further the equalizing effect of teacher influence.

When the equivalent-groups method was decided upon, the additional requirement was that subjects be selected and placed in the two groups in such a way that the resulting groups would really be equivalent.   To be equivalent the groups had to have like means and like variability among the subjects constituting each group; therefore, for every subject in one group, there was an equivalent subject in the other group, and it was so arranged that there was an equal number of subjects in each group.

This equivalence was not secured by chance, since there was too much danger of a constant tendency to make one group superior to the other.   The director of the experiment recognized that the best policy is to equate on the initial status of the subjects in the trait or traits in question; but this policy did not seem practical to use with the beginning first graders.   All the reading tests seemed too advanced for measurement purposes.   Reading tests for this purpose were given to just a few of the first grade pupils who knew how to read when they entered school; but these children were not included when the final equating was done.   In several of the classrooms equivalence was secured by equating on the basis of mental ages obtained by applying to the pupils the Detroit First Grade Intelligence Test [1] for beginning first grade pupils.   This test was administered by a trained tester to from four to eight pupils at a time so that there could be careful supervision and directions could

[1] Prepared by Anna M. Engel (World Book Company, Yonkers-on-Hudson, N. Y.).

be followed accurately; this procedure was considered necessary with children as immature as those beginning first grade. The content of the test given was compared with the Park-Franzen Test [2] made to measure readiness of pupils to do first grade work, and it was found that many of the items on the two tests are similar. Also, many of the items of the Detroit Test are similar to those of the Metropolitan Readiness Tests for Kindergarten and Grade 1. [3] It seems reasonable to conclude that the Detroit Test does measure some aptitude in reading among the following tests: (1) foundational information, (2) noting similarities of objects, (3) remembering a list of directions to be followed, (4) noting absurdities, (5) comparing sizes of objects, (6) seeing relationships between objects and their uses, (7) seeing a harmonious relation of parts, (8) holding in mind and reproducing designs, (9) counting, and (10) following directions. If this supposition is wise, then the Detroit First Grade Intelligence Test was a good one to use for the purpose. The pupils in three other small classes were equated on mental ages derived from the Stanford-Binet tests.

It seems reasonable to suppose that attendance is a determiner of skill in learning to read, and therefore this factor also was used for gaining equivalence.

Finally, the experimental set-up of the present study was determined by the fact that, on the whole, the equivalent-groups method is peculiarly free from the influence of disturbing irrelevant factors; and equivalence of groups was gained by the use of tests which determined mental ages on a series of tests closely resembling those used to determine aptitude in reading and readiness for first grade. Close attention was given to school attendance.

CONDITIONS OF THE EXPERIMENT

ORGANIZATION OF THE EXPERIMENT

Duration of the Experiment. Since this study deals with so important a matter as the effects of a new way of writing on beginning reading, it seemed necessary to spend one full school year on the investiga-

---

[2] Park-Franzen Test of Readiness of Pupils to Do First Grade Work. Oakland Public Schools, Bureau of Curriculum Development, Research and Guidance, Oakland, California.

[3] Hildreth, Gertrude H. and Griffiths, Nellie L., Metropolitan Readiness Tests for Kindergarten and Grade 1 (World Book Company, Yonkers-on-Hudson, N. Y., 1932).

tion.   Therefore, after the preliminary tests had been given and the
equating of subjects completed, the experiment proper started
about October 10, 1931, and continued for at least seven full, uninterrupted school months (until about May 20, 1932).

Communities Chosen.   The character of this study necessitated
close supervision and accurate and detailed observation by the
person in charge; and so, certain localities were selected not only
because they were conducive to worth-while results but also because
they were sufficiently near at hand to make possible frequent visits
by the director of the experiment.   Then, too, these communities
had taken part in the control division of the Wood-Freeman investigation and were therefore interested in the present undertaking.
Also, typewriters could be obtained easily.   The school systems had
good recognized reputations and the administrators [4] were progressive and open-minded; and they were eager to cooperate after
they understood the purposes and attending requirements of the
investigation.   The localities thus chosen were Elizabeth, New
Jersey, and the demonstration school at Teachers College, Columbia
University, New York City.

Class Distributions of Experimental and Control Pupils.   Table 1 shows
the class distribution of Experimental and Control children based
on the total enrollment and also on the final equating used for the
study of results.   Other facts, discussed below, are included.
Throughout the study the cities will be referred to by Roman
numerals, the schools by letters, and the classes by Arabic numerals.
The symbols X or T will indicate the Typewriter group and the
symbol C, the Control group.

Selection of Subjects and Teachers.   As a supplement to the experiment by Wood and Freeman, which had already found general
results with large numbers of pupils in first grade reading, this investigation called for a close and intensified study of effects on detailed phases of reading or on multiple abilities in reading.   A
minute study of happenings with a smaller group of subjects, as
scientifically controlled as possible, was the major aim.   Therefore
it would not have been of primary importance to have large numbers of children in this experiment.   A beginning number of 250
pupils, with about 125 subjects in each group, was needed.

---

[4] The principals who took part in the experiment were: Miss Isabelle Jane
Cameron, Mrs. May de Raismes, Miss Bessie Gallaher, Miss Florence Mason,
Miss Katherine E. Owen, Dr. Rollo G. Reynolds.

TABLE 1

Number of Schools, Teachers, and Pupils with Intelligence Quotient Ranges and Averages of Pupils and Distribution of Pupils and Typewriters within Classrooms

City	School	Class	No. of Teachers	No. of Pupils Enrolled in Each Group*		No. Pupils	I. Q. Range	Mean I. Q.	No. of Typewriters
				X†	C				
I	A	1	1	9	10	18	95–138	119.89	10
		2	1	9	9	12	101–129	118.92	
		3	1	8	8	12	104–136	121.50	
II	B	4	1	14	15	26	74–124	101.80	16
		5	1	16	17	30	81–123	107.57	
	C	6	1	21	23	42	77–131	101.69	14
	D	7	1	8	10	12	81–141	102.50	4
	E	8	1	13	14	26	71–113	87.00	15
		9	1	14	17	28	79–118	98.57	
	F	10	1	11	12	20	81–146	100.45	6
Total	6	10	10	123	135	226			65

* The numbers of pupils indicated in column 5 represent the initial enrollment for the different Experimental and Control groups in September, 1931. Some of these pupils were not included in the final equating and hence are not represented in column 6. Columns 7 and 8 represent the intelligence quotient ranges and averages for the pupils listed in column 6. The number of typewriters allotted to the Experimental pupils in each school are shown in the last column at the right.

† In this and the tables that follow, X indicates the Experimental group and C the Control group.

The selection of teachers and particular classrooms was the next consideration. Administrators and supervisors selected the particular schools and the individual teachers, keeping in mind that there was no desire for an outstandingly superior or inferior population in any respect and that the teachers, besides being qualified as first grade teachers, needed to be interested but unbiased, willing to cooperate, and capable of doing scientific work. The teachers selected on the basis of these criteria were interviewed by the director of the experiment, and the purposes of the experiment, the mechanical set-up, the procedures, and the particular obligations of the teachers in charge were explained to them. Their willingness to participate was expressed; and, in nearly every instance, an interested desire to cooperate was apparent. In this way five schools were selected, including seven first grade classrooms from Elizabeth, New Jersey, and three classes in the demonstration school, Teachers College, Columbia University.

Homogeneity of Teachers Selected.   The ratings of these teachers as skilled and successful first grade teachers did not, of course, indicate that they were alike in every respect.   There were individual differences in philosophy, personality, methods and procedures in teaching, amount of training, experience, and other factors, just as there are always differences in any group, no matter how homogeneous. Our main concern was the selection of teachers known by their supervisors or superiors to be able to gain good results and progressive in their outlook.   So if any teacher did not rank comparatively high in years of training, for instance, she was likely to rank very high in another factor, perhaps in educative experiences in her work or in special aptitude to meet her teaching problems; the summation of all her qualities and characteristics made her a well-qualified first grade teacher.

Homogeneity of Reading Instruction among Teachers.   It was not considered effective or feasible that all first grade teachers should attempt to teach reading in the same way.   However, in the selection of school systems and teachers, some attempt was made to avoid extreme differences among teachers in general principles of teaching reading and not to include in the experiment those who followed out-worn, antiquated methods and aims.   Just as both school systems are considered progressive in their general trends, so were the methods of teaching reading in the first grade found, in the main, to be progressive.   In City I (see Table 1), although no two teachers taught reading exactly alike, they were qualified to act as demonstration teachers for graduate students at Teachers College.   In City II the teachers followed in general the course of study in reading for the first grade constructed in 1925 by Isobel Davidson.[5]   In addition, these teachers were found to be using some of the most modern reading materials and texts and were putting into practice procedures determined by some of the latest scientific studies.   Therefore, no interference with teacher initiative or procedures was exercised. Each teacher was to act as she normally would to solve the problems in reading found in her classroom.   Advice was given, however, by the director of the experiment whenever any teacher asked for it.

Homogeneity of School Populations.   The populations of the different schools differed somewhat.   Table 1 indicates the intelligence quotient range and the average intelligence quotient for each school.

[5] Davidson, Isobel and Anderson, Charles Joseph, *The Lincoln Readers* and *Reading Objectives* (Laurel Book Company, Chicago, 1925).

On the basis of Terman's classification the average of children in School A is superior, and in all the other schools the average is normal.[6]   School A was a demonstration school, whereas the rest were not; it was also the only private institution—the others were public schools.   In economic and social conditions and in educational background it was evident that School A was very good, School D was good, Schools F and B were average with variations, and Schools E and C were low average with a number of exceptions. No school, however, was far below average in these respects.

Table 2 shows the character of the different schools in City II so far as nationality and race were concerned.

Of the 184 pupils in these seven classes, 110 (including 16 Negroes) were free from foreign language influence; that is, they and their parents were born in the United States and English was spoken in the home.   Only 4 children in the entire group were born in a foreign country; they were attending different schools.   Both the mother and the father of 48 of them were born outside the United States; 23 had one parent only who was born in a foreign country. A foreign language was spoken in 49 of the homes.

Twelve of the 16 Negroes in the experiment were in School E, and this number was 22 per cent of that school's population used in this experiment.

The per cent of homes, among the population in the different schools, where foreign language was spoken mainly is important in determining the child's possible handicap in reading achievement. Table 3 shows what per cent of the population (children used in the experiment) in each school had such an influence.   It is evident that the children studied in Schools C and D had the most chances of being affected.   Those in Schools E and B had less of the influence, and the children studied in School F had the least chance of being affected by foreign language.   School A is not included in Table 2. since all the children were born in the United States, a foreign language was spoken in one home only, and all belonged to the white race.   Therefore the chances for any foreign language influence were so small that a detailed analysis was unnecessary.

An analysis of the number of children who had kindergarten experience shows that in School A about 98 per cent of the children had attended kindergarten; in the other schools from 74 to 83 per cent had had kindergarten training.   Table 4 shows the number

[6] Terman, Lewis M., *The Measurement of Intelligence*, p. 79.

TABLE 2

Nationality and Racial Background of Pupils and Parents in Classes Studied in City II

School and Class	Number of Children	Country in Which Foreign Child Was Born	Country in Which Foreign Mother Was Born	Country in Which Foreign Father Was Born	Foreign Language Spoken at Home*
School B, Class 4	1	England	England	England	
	1		Austria	Austria	Austrian
	1		Greece	Greece	Greek
	1		Rumania	Rumania	Rumanian
	1		Scotland	Scotland	
	1		Austria		
	2		France		
	1		Rumania		
	2			Austria	
	1			Hungary	
	1			Ireland	
	2			Russia	Hebrew
	1			Norway	
	10	American-born children with native-born parents. English spoken in the home.			
	26				
School B, Class 5	1		Austria	Austria	Austrian
	1		Denmark	Denmark	Danish
	1		England	Russia	
	3		Russia	Russia	Hebrew
	1		Austria		
	1		France		
	1			Czecho-slovakia	
	1			Russia	
	1				Hebrew
	19	American-born children with native-born parents. English spoken in the home.			
	30				
School C, Class 6	1	Germany	Germany	Germany	German
	1		Austria	Austria	Hebrew
	4		Czecho-slovakia	Czecho-slovakia	Slavic
	2		England	England	
	3		Germany	Germany	German
	5		Italy	Italy	Italian
	2		Russia	Russia	Hebrew
	2		Scotland	Scotland	
	1				Hebrew
	21	American-born children with native-born parents. English spoken in the home.			
	42				

TABLE 2 (*Continued*)

School and Class	Number of Children	Countries in Which Foreign Children Were Born	Countries in Which Foreign Mothers Were Born	Countries in Which Foreign Fathers Were Born	Foreign Language Spoken at Home
School D, Class 7	1	Italy	Italy	Italy	Italian
	1		Germany	Germany	German
	1		Russia	Russia	Hebrew
	1		Sweden	Sweden	Swedish
	1		Canada		
	1				Hebrew
	6	American-born children with native-born parents. English spoken in the home.			
	12				
School E, Class 8	1	Italy	Italy	Italy	Italian
	2		Scotland	Scotland	
	1		Canada		
	1		Germany		
	21	American-born children with native-born parents (including 10 Negroes). English spoken in the home.			
	26				
School E, Class 9	1		Austria	Austria	Austrian
	3		Germany	Germany	German
	3		Italy	Italy	Italian
	2		Russia	Russia	Hebrew
	2			Russia	Hebrew
	17	American-born children with native-born parents (including 2 Negroes). English spoken in the home.			
	28				
School F, Class 10	1		Germany	Germany	German
	1			Italy	Italian
	2			Russia	Hebrew
	16	American-born children with native-born parents (including 4 Negroes). English spoken in the home.			
	20				

* This column indicates the particular foreign language spoken in certain homes.

and per cent of children in the classes studied who had had kindergarten training, and the amount of the training. One term in these schools is equivalent in length to a period of four and one-half to five months.

TABLE 3

Per Cent of Pupils in Classes Studied in City II Having: Both Parents of Foreign Birth, One Parent Only Foreign Born, and Foreign Language Spoken at Home

Classification	Percentage of Children in School				
	B	C	D	E	F
Both parents of foreign birth..........	20	50	33	22	5
Only one parent foreign born..........	26	..	8	8	15
Foreign language spoken at home......	20	40	42	22	20

TABLE 4

Number and Per Cent of Children Who Had Attended Kindergarten

School	Number Having Kindergarten Experience		Per Cent Having Kindergarten Experience
	2 Terms	1 Term	
A........................	41	..	98%
B........................	37	8	80
C........................	26	9	83
D........................	5	4	75
E........................	28	12	74
F........................	12	4	80

PREPARATION FOR TYPEWRITING INSTRUCTION

Number and Types of Machines. Sixty-five portable typewriters were lent by four leading manufacturing companies (Corona, Remington, Royal, and Underwood) for the purposes of the experiment. On the average there was one typewriter for every two pupils in the Experimental group. These machines were equipped with primer type so that they would be better suited to the ocular perception of first grade children. In the course of the Wood-Freeman study it was observed that general confusion among first grade children resulted when the key caps of the typewriter were covered with capital letters, as is generally done; the children failed to see why one should strike a capital letter and get a small letter. Then, too, the capital letters were very different from those on the printed pages of their books. This difficulty was easily overcome in the present study by covering the key caps with lower case letters before the experiment was begun.

Care of Machines.   To prevent injury or loss of machines, arrangements were made in the various rooms for cabinets or cupboards in which typewriters could be locked and kept when not in use. Teachers, but no children, were allowed to take a typewriter from the school building.   A typewriter service man was near by to inspect machines regularly and to give mechanical attention on short notice.   Teachers were asked to request the services of this mechanic whenever typewriters were in need of adjustment.

Teachers' Acquaintance with Typewriting.   Of the six classes which were instructed by teachers who knew how to use the typewriter when the experiment started, three of these groups were taught by teachers who had completed a typewriting course; one was taught by a skilled typist; and the remaining two classes had teachers possessing sufficient skill to do typewriting for everyday purposes.   With the four remaining teachers, who could not do typing, it was emphasized that sufficient skill in typewriting for purposes of instruction in the first grade could be attained in a short time.   Accordingly a scheme for learning typewriting, suggested by Mrs. Josephine Ambrose, teacher of typewriting in the Horace Mann School, together with the necessary materials and charts, was given these four teachers at the opening of the school session, several weeks before the experiment proper was begun.   The teachers cooperated to such a degree that at the beginning of the experiment even the most unskilled teacher knew how to use the important general features of the typewriter: shift key, back spacer, space bar, paper release, paper holder, single and double space device, and margin stops.   They had had sufficient practice to be able to start typewriting instruction of first grade children with the aid of the guidance which was furnished them.

Avoidance of Typewriting by Control Children.   The equating of children within a classroom where typewriters were to be used by one group while the other group was required not to use them, led to an anticipation of a keen desire on the part of Control pupils to use the machines.   In order to avoid any disastrous effects on experimental results certain precautions were taken.   Care was taken to select for Control groups children who had not used the typewriter previously, either at home or in the kindergarten.   In communities where there was likelihood that typewriters were in the homes, a letter was sent to the parents of Control pupils asking that they cooperate by not granting the privilege of the use of the machine to the child while the study was in progress.

A copy of a letter sent to parents in one community is reproduced here:

To the Parents of First Grade Children:

Perhaps you have heard of the introduction of the typewriter as an instrument of expression in some schools, including . . . . School. Since this is a new movement, careful investigations have been made and are being carried on to determine scientifically its effects and the best way to use the typewriter in our schools. . . . . School is a part of such an investigation.

This year we are eager to find out what are the effects, good or bad, of the use of the typewriter in the first grade. At the present time we do not know whether the typewriter is a help or a hindrance in this grade. If it is a help, we need to know it. Therefore we seek your cooperation in a scientific experiment during most of the school year. During this time only half of the pupils, selected in an unbiased and scientific way, are to use the typewriters. The other half are not to use them at school, at home, or anywhere else. While one group is typing, the other group will go on with the regular work of the grade, engaging in a variety of interesting activities. This group, however, may use the typewriters during the latter part of the year after the period of investigation has terminated; and they can look forward to the use of them next year. The main point we wish to emphasize with parents is that typewriters should not be used in the home by the children who are not to use them at school.

We assure you we will use every effort to give first consideration to the welfare of your child, and we thank you for your cooperation.

Yours sincerely

Principal of the School

TYPES OF EVIDENCE

Keeping in mind that the purpose of this study is to find out detailed effects on beginning reading and also to note accurately under what conditions these effects were produced, these types of evidence were depended upon mainly:

1. Test Results. Results from tests administered to all pupils in Experimental and Control groups in early January, 1932, and in late May, 1932 (with several exceptions).

> a. Gates Primary Reading Tests to measure ability to read for thought.
>> (a) Type I, Word Recognition, to measure ability to read words representative of the primary vocabulary. (This test was given in the early part of December.)
>> (b) Type II, Word, Phrase, and Sentence Reading, to measure ability to read verbal units of increasing complexity.
>> (c) Type III, Paragraph Reading, to measure ability to read and comprehend complete paragraphs.

b. Haggerty Reading Examination, Sigma 1, to measure abilities: (1) to read and comprehend paragraphs, and (2) to read and comprehend sentences.

c. Detroit Word Recognition Test to measure ability to recognize words.

d. Gray's Oral Reading Test (1) to measure ability in oral reading, (2) to determine nature of difficulties in oral reading, (3) to detect phonetic and other analytic skills in the process of reading; to ascertain to what extent the pupil can utilize the context as an aid in the recognition of words and to what extent certain other methods of word recognition function in the actual process of reading, (4) to determine rate of oral reading. (Given to School A only in January; given to all schools in May.)

e. Gates Visual Perception Tests.

(a) Test A1—(given in January only) to measure ability to see small objects or figures more or less similar to words: to note similarities or dissimilarities of items.

(b) Test A3—to measure ability to see printed words and to note their similarities and dissimilarities.

(c) Test B2—(given in May only) to measure ability to see printed letters and words: to note their similarities and dissimilarities and to select one among many for matching.

f. Gates' Phonetic Ability Tests (given to pupils in School A only) to measure ability to recognize and deal in certain ways with individual word elements.

g. Gates' Pronunciation Test (given to pupils in School A only) to measure ability to pronounce words in isolation and to note method of attack on pronunciation.

h. Typewriting Tests for First Grade which had been constructed as a part of the Wood-Freeman experiment to measure speed and accuracy in typewriting.

2. Concrete Data and Observation. Concrete data and observations which help to describe reading abilities were obtained as follows:

a. In January and in May, during a "free period" of 30 minutes, each teacher recorded the names of children who chose reading as an activity.

b. A record of the number and names of books read by each child during the year was kept by the teachers.

3. Teachers' Judgments. A valuable source of information concerning reading abilities of pupils in the first grade comes from the teacher. Accordingly, a letter was sent to the teachers who took part in the experiment, asking for their judgments of the pupils' reading abilities. Following are two extracts from these letters:

"I need to have your rating of general reading ability of each child at this time [May 23]. Please give ratings in terms of: A—Excellent;

B—Above average; C—Your conception of average first grade ability at this time; D—Below average; E—Failing.

"Besides this, a short paragraph of statements about each child's growth in reading ability is desired. I am asking that this include items like the following: interest in reading—effort put forth in learning to read—background of experiences—home influence—good or poor powers of concentration—eyesight—health—dependence on memory—immaturity—social adjustment—evidence of dislike for symbols—overemphasis of words—speech defects—language handicap—ability to attack new word independently—eye span—phonetic ability—attack on words (initial sounds, endings, general configuration, or context)—ability to get thought—vocabulary. Will you please comment on the items needed to characterize each case?"

Just the general ratings in items of A, B, C, D, and E were given in January. In May both the quantitative plus the qualitative reports described in the letter were collected.

4. Children's Typewritten Materials. In order to perceive accurately the relationship between typewriting and reading in the first grade it was essential to examine the writings on the typewriter of each child who was using the machine to note not only the quantity and quality of work done but also its nature and character. All the typewritten materials of each child were collected in a separate folder by the teacher in charge. Each piece of material was dated before it was placed in the file.

5. Record of Control Pupils' Activities. Teachers were asked to keep an accurate account of what the Control group was doing while the Typewriter group was typing, in terms of: time spent on the activity, explanation of the activity, accomplishments. Whenever possible, samples of work done were saved to show what had been accomplished. A study of these records revealed what activities and accomplishments had to be omitted in the life of the Experimental child because he did not have the time for them. They also were compared with accomplishments on the typewriter in the light of their apparent effects on reading.

PROCEDURE

Efforts were made to conduct the experiment strictly according to the plans formulated, while constant consideration was being given to the child's welfare and to the school's and community's needs.

Controlling Activities of Both Groups. One of the most important considerations had to do with freeing both groups from disturbing factors which might create inaccuracy in results. The program of activities for the Control group was equivalent to what it would have been if no experiment had been in progress; at the same time an accurate record was kept by the teacher to show what the Control pupils did while the other group was typing. The program of activities for the Experimental group was equivalent to what it normally would have been, with the exception that from 75 to 90 minutes per week were used for typewriting. The need for flexibility in a first grade program was realized; yet a plan of organization had to be followed for the sake of a scientific study. It meant that, to more of an extent than is adovcated ordinarily, a preview of time allotments for different types of activities was needed. The following extract from a letter sent in October to the ten teachers [7] who took part in the experiment explains the plan for controlling the activities of the Control and Experimental groups:

"Suppose that typewriting is to be added as an activity to an already carefully planned grade program which has every period taken up with required activities carefully apportioned on the basis of importance in time allotments. We cannot drop from the schedule any type of activity because each is important; nor should we take away an unproportional amount from any subject, because the time for each has already been allotted on the basis of importance. The thing to do, then, is to divide the total number of classroom minutes per week by the total number of minutes to be used weekly for typewriting. For example, if there were 1,200 minutes in the school week and 60 minutes of this time were devoted to typing, we would say that 1/20 of the time is being utilized for this activity. Therefore 1/20 of the time ordinarily used for each activity is to be used for typing. Suppose for example, that the following program has been in operation before typewriting is introduced:

A Fictitious Example of a First Grade Program

Activity	Number of Minutes per Week
Individual and group (with access to shop, studio, and science room)	320
Group meetings	100
Outdoor play and indoor play in gymnasium	160
Luncheon and rest	160
Language arts and skills	340
Music	80
Assembly	40
Total	1,200

[7] Miss Agnes Burke, Miss Mary M. Hopkins, Miss Melany Irek, Mrs. Mabel Meadowcroft, Miss Jane Mingo, Miss Evelyn Phillips, Mrs. Henriette Snyder, Miss Ethel Spurr, Mrs. Marie Traynor, Miss Catharine Wellman.

"Typing is to demand 60 minutes per week, which is 1/20 of the total time. Therefore, 1/20 of the time on each subject must be subtracted from the original time allotted to it.   1/20 of 320 = 16 and 320 − 16 = 304 minutes to be given to individual and group activities; 1/20 of 100 = 5 and 100 − 5 = 95 minutes to be given to group meetings; 1/20 of 160 = 8 and 160 − 8 = 152 minutes to be given to play and to luncheon and rest respectively; 1/20 of 340 = 17 and 340 − 17 = 323 minutes to be given to language arts and skills; 1/20 of 80 = 4 and 80 − 4 = 76 minutes to be given to music; lastly, 1/20 of 40 = 2 and 40 − 2 = 38 minutes to be given to assembly.   The program on a weekly basis would follow thus:

A Fictitious Example of the Program of a First Grade Involved in the Experiment

Activity	Number of Minutes per Week	
	X Group	C Group
Individual and group....................	304	304
Group meetings........................	95	95
Play.................................	152	152
Luncheon and rest......................	152	152
Language arts and skills.................	323	323
Music...............................	76	76
Assembly............................	38	38
Total............................	1,140	1,140
Typewriting..........................	60	
Individual and group....................		16
Group meetings........................		5
Play.................................		8
Luncheon and rest......................		8
Language arts and skills.................		17
Music...............................		4
Assembly............................		2
Grand total........................	1,200	1,200

"Our programs should be arranged according to the latter scheme. The Control and Experimental groups will not be working as separate groups except during periods when the Experimental group is typing; then the Control group should be engaging in the activities of the ordinary school program in amounts as equivalent as possible to the amount of time subtracted for typewriting. Thus, so far as time allotments per subject are concerned, the program of the Control group will remain unchanged."

For nearly every classroom, the director of this experiment examined the existing program and rearranged it on a monthly basis in terms of the plan suggested.

The teachers cooperated in keeping an accurate account of what the Control group was doing while the Experimental group was typing, in terms of: time spent on activity; an explanation of the activity; accomplishments. At frequent intervals, unless the supervisor of the experiment had reasons for feeling certain that a well-regulated program was being followed, these reports were collected and examined to see whether the different activities of the first grade program were being engaged in proportionately. The report that follows is an example of the typical monthly report which was investigated. It indicates what was done by one Control group during the month of February. Typewriting was engaged in by the Experimental division of this class during three thirty-minute periods per week.

FEBRUARY 1—30 minutes

Children filled in right numbers in squares:

Addition:

2	2	☐	3	3	☐	1	1	☐
2	☐	2	1	☐	1	3	☐	3
—	—	—	—	—	—	—	—	—
☐	4	4	☐	4	4	☐	4	4

Discussion about the correct answers followed the work period.

FEBRUARY 3—30 minutes.

Children did what the directions on the blackboard told them to do:
Make a picture of Nan.*
Make a picture of Nan's doll.
Make a picture of Nan's pet.

FEBRUARY 5—30 minutes.

Music period—Pupils sang patriotic songs to get ready for school assembly.

FEBRUARY 8—30 minutes.

Children made enough patriotic badges so that each child could wear one to the assembly.*

FEBRUARY 10—30 minutes.

Children made original valentines for friends and parents. This work included:
Cutting the valentines.*
Drawing of pictures and designs.
Composing and copying greetings.

* A sample was enclosed.

FEBRUARY 12—30 minutes.

The work of February 10 was continued.   Some of the greetings were:

"Ho, ho, Valentine!"

"I want you to be my Valentine."

"Will you be my Valentine?"

FEBRUARY 15—30 minutes.

Children made a shelf for articles to be put in the museum.

FEBRUARY 17—30 minutes.

Stories were read to the children and discussions arose.

FEBRUARY 19—30 minutes.

Teacher gave children their new primer, *Peter and Peggy*.   They read two pages and loved it.

FEBRUARY 24—30 minutes.

Number game.

Children played in groups of three.   One group had large cards containing groups of figures; another group had word cards; and the third group had number cards.

They matched cards like this:

. ˙ .		3		Three

FEBRUARY 26—30 minutes.

Children washed the dishes after a birthday party.

FEBRUARY 29—30 minutes.

Children dramatized "The King's Breakfast."   This called for some reading.

If a scrutiny of any of these reports led the director of the experiment to believe that a poor control of activities was being exercised, conferences were held with the teacher to determine how better regulation could be exercised at the least sacrifice of flexibility and integration of activities and of essential needs inherent in the group. At certain periods allowances had to be made; for example, in one class most attention for a period of three or four weeks had to be given to the production of a spring pageant.   This called for special emphasis on reading and gathering information to gain ideas, composition of speech parts, dancing, singing, designing and making of costumes, and practice in assembling all parts for the effect desired. At that time the usual amount of emphasis was not given to arithmetic, typewriting, certain types of reading, and other elements of the program.   The unit of work following the pageant, however, called for sufficient emphasis upon these activities to compensate previous losses. On the yearly basis, it was felt that in every classroom a well-controlled regulation of activities was in effect for experimental purposes and each type of activity was developed to meet the needs of the pupils involved in both groups.

Typewriting Instruction. The typewriting instruction combined a formal method for the purpose of developing technical abilities to use the machine with an informal method for teaching the children to use the machine in purposeful first grade situations.

A systematic scheme for teaching typewriting in the first grade, formulated by Dr. Ralph Haefner [8] as a result of two years of experimentation with over 700 first grade children, was placed in the hands of each teacher. This arrangement of exercises was followed as closely as possible. The exercises started with the writing of words selected from the list of the first five hundred words of the Gates graded word list. These words were selected carefully after due consideration of their degree of difficulty in writing, so that techniques and skills could be developed step by step in proper order. Then phrases were introduced, followed by sentences. On each page were appropriate illustrations to accompany the words, phrases, or sentences. Also, on each page were directions to be read to the children, explaining what was to be written, which hand was to be used, and similar instructions.

At the same time emphasis was laid on the fact that the typewriter is an *instrument of expression.* When the typewriter was introduced, the children were led to see that it could be used for writing purposes. Many children were eager to do actual writing at once. Some wrote their names or other words the first time they sat down to the machine. The use of the machine for immediate, meaningful writing is the most obvious response to make. For this reason sufficient encouragement and opportunity were given so that pupils would use the typewriters for whatever purposeful writing they wished to do. Some of this was original and some was copied. Here are examples of the types of writing:

Writing names.
Copying from books, blackboard, or other sources.
Typing notices for the bulletin board.
Writing words from memory.
Writing greetings.
Typing individual or group compositions for booklets, or charts.

[8] *Typewriting Exercises for First Grade.*

Typing individual or group letters to be sent to others.

Writing numbers in chronological order.

Writing the date on papers to be handed in.

Writing characters other than the alphabet and numbers.

Creative writing of sentences, poems, and prose composition.

All the writings of each child were kept in his individual folder.

The children who used typewriters were placed in a situation that was conducive to learning respect for property. They were shown that the typewriter is an expensive machine and that the repair work is costly. They were led to see that the typewriter is an instrument for writing purposes rather than a toy. In one instance a professional typist talked to the class about her attitude and feeling toward her typewriter; she spoke of it as one of her treasures, of the services it renders her every day because she understands it and treats it with care, of the delicacy of its parts, which can be broken easily through misuse or lack of understanding. When an attitude of respect had been developed, in nearly every case children were cautious about trying to use any part of the machine until they had learned how. As the work progressed they were cautioned against pressing more than one key at a time, playing with the ribbon reverse, returning the carriage with a bang, dropping the machine, moving the machine before it was closed tightly, and other careless acts. The difficult processes involved in opening and closing machines, locking and unlocking the carriage, replacing the cover, and other processes were learned gradually. Only the larger children were allowed to carry the machines, and then for short distances only.

The synopsis that follows of the exact happenings of one group of nine children shows some of the teaching problems encountered and how they were met in this particular case. There was an average of three typewriting periods weekly, varying in length from twenty to thirty minutes. The typewriters were always placed in position for writing before the children started to use them. Sheets of plain white paper $5\frac{1}{2}''$ x $8\frac{1}{2}''$ in size were used.

SUMMARY OF LESSONS FOR ONE GROUP

Lesson 1. In a discussion period these ideas were developed:

1. That the typewriter can be used for writing purposes.
2. That it costs a great deal.
3. That its machinery is complex and delicate, causing it to be damaged easily.

The children learned to remove the covers and to place them in safe places.

Lesson 2. Through explanation, demonstration, and actual doing, these processes were learned:

1. How to insert and remove the paper.
2. How to push the carriage into position for writing.

Lesson 3. The children inserted paper and pushed the carriage into position for writing. Then, using the first finger of each hand, they practiced striking alternatingly any of the keys with an even stroke and a staccato touch until the bell rang. The carriage was then brought into position for a new line. The purpose of this was to develop a sharp, snappy, even touch. The children noticed that striking keys made letters on the paper. Using the proper finger for making the letter h, they wrote a line of this letter with an effort at using a desirable stroke. Using the proper finger, a line of g's was made also. The children were thus led to discover that the letter struck on the keyboard produces a corresponding letter on the paper. With this idea in mind they tried writing their names. All accomplished fair results; and three children, without guidance, made the capitals where they belonged.

Lesson 4. Again machines were opened, paper was inserted, and the carriage was pushed into proper position for writing. The papers of the three children who wrote their names with capitals were examined by the other children, and they decided that the capital letters made the names look better. The other children wished to learn to use capitals.

Drill was given on making the capital M with one hand and the capital V with the other, using the correct fingers. The pupils all made successful attempts to apply this knowledge to the writing of their names.

Lesson 5. On this day the instructor showed the children colored labels which were ready to be pasted on individual folders for holding typewritten materials as soon as names could be written upon them. Names correctly written during the last period were examined, and the children were led to notice the fact that each word started with a capital and that there was a space between each two words. Every child tried to write his name. Two of the names had to be written on the blackboard first to show correct spelling. After individual pupils had written their names correctly, the labels were given to them. Stanton, Wilbur, and Jean wrote their names on labels.   Others almost finished theirs.   In the time left Stanton and Wilbur tried writing numbers and other characters.

Lesson 6.   Today Stanton, Wilbur, and Jean chose to write the following verses, which had been composed and read in class:

> Over the housetops in the sky
> Who saw the Akron sailing by?
> I   I   I   I   I
> I saw the Akron sailing by.

Stanton wrote the most; he wrote, "Over the housetops in" without a mistake.

After practice Mary and Gertrude seemed ready to write names on labels.

Lesson 7.   Drill was given on writing the word *milk* over and over again with the right hand and with a space between words. Names were written on papers.

Lesson 8.   Earl, Gertrude, Mary, Larry, and Mildred practiced writing their names.   Mildred and Mary seemed ready to write names on labels.   The rest practiced writing *milk*.

Lesson 9.   Sheet number 1 [9] was used this morning as a drill exercise.   All the pupils wrote their names on papers; one boy needed much help.   Margaret wrote her name on the label without a mistake, and then continued writing the Akron poem.

Lesson 10.   Sheet number 2 was used for drill.   Names were written on papers; two children needed much help.

Lesson 11.   Sheet number 3 was used for drill.   Names were written on papers.

Lesson 12.   Five children had not written names on labels, so their interest was enlisted in doing this.   Larry and Gertrude succeeded in doing it successfully.   Mary showed that she needed more practice.   Earl and August practiced also.   The rest of the children continued writing the Akron poem; Wilbur wrote it all correctly except the last word, by.

Lesson 13.   Today was Pauline's and Wilbur's birthday.   The following were composed and written by the children:

> Happy birthday to Pauline.
> Happy birthday to Wilbur.
> Today is Wilbur's birthday.
> Today is Pauline's birthday.

[9] Drill exercises referred to in Lessons 9 to 74 inclusive were constructed by Dr. Ralph Haefner.

Six out of nine children had sentences perfectly written so that they could present them to Pauline or to Wilbur.

Lesson 14. Sheet number 4 was used for drill. All the children except Larry accomplished a great deal. Gertrude, Stanton, and Wilbur had time to write whatever they wished. Wilbur wrote his name many times. Gertrude wrote *bed* and *milk* many times. Stanton wrote *milk* many times.

Lesson 15. Mary, Earl, and August practiced writing their names for labels; Mary and Earl succeeded.

The rest of the children composed and wrote from a blackboard copy:

> We are going to the assembly.
> We will see farm animals.

Larry, Stanton, and Jean wrote perfect copies of this, which were placed on the class bulletin board.

Lesson 16. Sheet number 5 was used as a drill exercise, writing the word *cat* with the left hand only. Then names were written on papers.

Lesson 17. Drill on sheet number 6 involved the use of both hands; but most of the children, in a short time, wrote only a line or two. Names were written on papers.

Lesson 18. Sheet number 6 was finished. Very good work was done.

Lesson 19. The school typist was visited. In a discussion following the visit, these observations were emphasized: She wrote with speed; she used both hands and all her fingers. A chart showing the different fingers to use on different keys was examined.

The children decided to write the greeting:

> Merry Christmas
> and
> A Happy New Year.

The greeting was written on the blackboard and the pupils learned how to read it.

Lesson 20. Christmas and New Year's greetings were written. Everyone did very well.

Lesson 21. Sheet number 7 was used for drill. Names were written on papers.

Lesson 22. Each child was told to write whatever he wished. These items were typewritten by the pupils after copies had been written on the blackboard:

Merry Christmas
and
A Happy New Year.

_____

Merry Christmas
to
Mommy and Daddy.

_____

Our Christmas Party.

_____

Earl brought a kiddie car.
Bobby brought a pair of stockings.

_____

family.

Lesson 23. The children did sheet number 8 for drill purposes. Wrote names on papers.

Lesson 24. An opportunity was given the children to write whatever they wished. The following were written after a copy was put on the board:

1. milk—cat—dog—hoop—car.
2. A Happy Christmas.
3. Merry Christmas.
4. Happy birthday to Jean.
5. Merry Christmas to Miss Blank.
6. Merry Christmas and A Happy New Year.

Lesson 25. All wrote Merry Christmas to fathers, mothers, friends, and servants. They took their greetings with them.

Lesson 26. New Year's greetings were written and pasted on cards. The greeting was:

A Happy New Year 1932

The greeting was written correctly by all individuals from one to three times.

Lesson 27. The children did sheet number 9 for drill purposes. They also wrote names on papers.

Lesson 28. Today the children were allowed to choose whatever they wished to write. Most of them chose to write notes, words, or letters written previously.

Lesson 29. The children did sheet number 10 for drill purposes. They also wrote names on papers.

Lesson 30. Happenings of the week-end were discussed and it was decided that they would be of interest to the whole class. This led to the suggestion that pieces of news from time to time should be typed and taken back to the class to be placed on the bulletin board. Today it was decided to type this piece of news:

> Jean . . . rode across the George Washington
> Bridge yesterday.

No copy was good enough to be posted; but some children nearly approached the standard.

Lesson 31. The children did sheet number 11 today for drill purposes. They also wrote names on papers.

Lesson 32. The children decided to rewrite the news item of the thirtieth lesson for a newspaper. Stanton's copy was written without a mistake and was accepted by the class for the newspaper.

Lesson 33. A typewriting test for speed and accuracy was administered.

Lesson 34. Valentine greetings which had been composed in class were written on the blackboard at the request of the children. There were three different greetings:

> Valentine, Valentine
> Will you be my Valentine?
>
> ———
>
> Ho! Ho!
> Valentine time is here.
>
> ———
>
> You can't get away
> from me—my Valentine.

Mary and Wilbur each had a perfect copy of the first greeting.

Lesson 35. The children continued writing Valentine greetings. Two new abilities were developed:

> 1. Writing an exclamation mark.
> 2. Writing the apostrophe.

One child did not complete a selection without mistakes, but the others each completed one or two or three. Wilbur and Mary did the best writing.

Lesson 36. The one child who was unsuccessful last time wrote the Valentine greetings correctly and took them with him. The rest of the children did sheet number 12 for practice purposes. They wrote their names on their papers.

Lesson 37. Four children chose to write Valentine verses and five chose to write the following news item:

> Larry goes to the Church of All Nations.
> From the big roof he can see the Empire
> State Building and the Chrysler Building.

Larry noticed that the word *church* ends as it starts, with *ch*.
Only part of this item was written by most of the children.*

* At the end of each lesson the part of the news items written without mistakes was cut out and pasted on the news sheet. From that point the writing of the composition was continued during a later period.

Lesson 38.   Sheet number 13 was written.   Names were written on the papers.   Some of the children had time left to write Valentine verses.

Lesson 39.   The children finished writing the news item started in the thirty-seventh lesson.   The part written today was:

> State Building and the Chrysler Building.

They wrote their names on papers.

Lesson 40.   Different members of the class read aloud the two newspaper items which were completed.   They decided to let the rest of the class see it.   Sheet number 14 was done for drill.   The children also wrote names on papers.

Lesson 41.   The children had just come from visiting the fire house; so they decided to write a "thank you" note to the captain.   This is the note which was composed and partly typewritten:

> Dear Captain Stack:
>   Thank you for the nice
> fun we had at your fire house.   We learned
> how to slide down the pole, how the alarm
> comes in, how to blow the siren, and how
> the firemen put on their hats,
>   Love from
>   Miss Blank's Class
>   . . . . School.

Lesson 42.   The children finished doing sheet number 14.   Those who finished before the end of the period wrote successfully this part of the letter to the firemen: "the nice fun we had at your firehouse. We learned how to slide down the pole, how the alarm comes in, how to."

Lesson 43.   The writing of the letter, which was composed in Lesson 41, was completed.   The last part was written on the board for the children to copy: "blow the siren, and how the firemen put on their hats.

> Love from
> Miss Blank's Class
> . . . . School.

Lesson 44. The children asked to typewrite any words which they knew how to spell. The words were not written on the black-board. The papers showed a variety of words.

Lesson 45. Sheet number 15 was done. Names and date were written on papers. August finished first and composed the news item:

> August's mother went to the country
> for Washington's birthday.

Those who finished the exercise first wrote part of the news item.

Lesson 46. The children finished the news item started last time, writing:

> country for Washington's birthday.
> She stayed three days and she played
> golf.

They also wrote the news item, "We made a fire alarm box."

Lesson 47. Time was taken to work out a scheme by which children would have their chances at using machines with red and black ribbons. They started exercise number 16 and wrote names on papers.

Lesson 48. Exercise number 16 was finished and names and dates were written on papers. Stanton said, "When you write *a t*, it says *at* and when you put a *c* back of it, it says *cat*."

Lesson 49. All wrote a verse composed in classroom:

> Wind blowing
> March!
> March winds are blowing.

Gertrude also wrote, "Happy Birthday from Gertrude."

The following news item was composed and some of the children made an effort to type it:

> Stanton, Wilbur, Jean, and Gertrude have
> gone to the 102nd floor of the Empire
> State Building.

Lesson 50. The children did exercise 17 and wrote names and date on papers. Stanton had time to continue the news item.

Lesson 51. The children finished the news item started in the forty-ninth lesson, "have gone to the 102nd floor of the Empire State Building."

Lesson 52. For twenty minutes the children typed all the words they knew from memory. Next the instructor dictated from a list of words which the children had collected in the classroom, and they typed those which they thought they knew how to spell. This shows what was written on the best paper, along with the name and date:

```
father  man  good  lady  too mother out
there was  see and   candy six bovx box
one for   much day bat eat cat dog at it
house a I am Valentine automobile said
red ate very two Stanton Roger dear god
God in my tom is Billy to the mill   hat
```

This shows what was written on the poorest paper, along with the name and date:

```
milk   Bibby cat bog bed canby Am AN Ann
meh hoop Fn! Fn!   Earl Earl Lary G Go
sews so goeistt Boppy to the thism mill
```

Lesson 53.   The children did sheet number 18 and wrote names and dates on papers.   Those who finished first wrote an announcement for the bulletin board:

Red Ribbons
March 9
Jean
Mary
Mildred

Lesson 54.   The following news item was composed and partly typewritten:

```
The boys and girls in Miss Blank's room are
making a museum.   They are making shelves and
backs to the shelves.   They will put things
like the Empire State Building and a shark's
tooth into the museum.
```

The name and date was written on each paper.

Lesson 55.   A typewriting test for speed and accuracy was administered.   The Hickory, Dickory, Dock selection was used.

Lesson 56.   Sheet number 19 was done for drill purposes.   The children wrote names and the date.

Lesson 57.   They finished typing the news item started in Lesson 54.

Lesson 58.   Sheet number 20 was done for drill purposes.   The children wrote names and dates on papers.

Lesson 59.   They wrote names and the dates on papers.   Then they composed and in part wrote on the typewriter the following news item:

> Some of us are going on trips during the
> Easter vacation. Wilbur is going to Atlantic
> City. Earl is going to Florida. Larry is
> going to Indian Point. Gertrude and August
> are going to the country.

Lesson 60. The children wrote names and dates on papers and did sheet number 21.

Lesson 61. They finished the news item started in Lesson 59, writing, "Indian Point. Gertrude and August are going to the country."

Lesson 62. They wrote names and the date on papers and did sheet number 22. The ones who finished early composed the following news item to be written next time:

> Wilbur and Earl were the ones who went away
> during Easter vacation.

Lesson 63. The work started late today. The children added to the composition of the news item started last time by writing, "Wilbur did go to Atlantic City. Earl went to Long Island and touched the Atlantic Ocean."

Lesson 64. A typewriting test was given, using the selection, "Playing Indians."

Lesson 65. Sheet number 23 was done. The children wrote names and the date, and did the exercises at the bottom of the page.

Lesson 66. The class composed the following news item and wrote it:

> We are making a battleship. It has
> windows and a pointed front. It is
> made out of wood.

Lesson 67. Sheet number 24 was done. The children wrote names and the date on papers.

Lesson 68. They composed a riddle about the typewriter and typed it to put on the bulletin board so that the rest of the class could guess what it was:

> What is it?
> It has letters and numbers.
> It has dots and question marks.
> It has much machinery.
> It has a ribbon.
> You can carry it.

Lesson 69. The children did sheet number 25 after the directions for it had been discussed fully. Wrote names and the date on papers.

Lesson 70.   The class decided to write another "riddle" for the rest of the class to guess:

"Why doesn't an elephant have long tusks?"

Jean, Stanton, and Wilbur had theirs written without mistakes, and so showed them to the rest of the class.

Lesson 71.   The children did part of sheet number 26.   The period was short.

Lesson 72.   They finished doing sheet number 26 and wrote names and the date.   Stanton composed this riddle:

Why do you wash your face before you
come to the table?

Several children wrote it.

Lesson 73.   The class composed and wrote this news item:

Wilbur and Gertrude are going to the country
on Saturday.   They will stay overnight and come
home on Sunday.

Lesson 74.   The children did sheet number 29.

Lesson 75.   A typewriting test for speed and accuracy was administered.

The plan of teaching typewriting used in this experiment is not presented as a model.   There were two definite handicaps: (1) lack of enough scientific study of previous typewriting teaching in the first grade to draw reliable conclusions concerning the best methods; (2) the experimental situation, which necessitated a control of the time element, materials used, a defined method, and the Experimental and Control groups within each classroom.   This situation naturally resulted in more artificiality and formality in the use of the machines than would be advocated for ordinary practice.   It is admitted that for these reasons there were sometimes limitations in using the typewriter to the fullest extent as an educational instrument in the classroom.   Although an effort was made to make the typewriting instruction as productive as possible of educational outcomes, nevertheless, as the study of this problem of teaching continues, results that are more productive can be expected.

Standards for First Grade.   During the experiment it was emphasized that first grade children should be held to no higher standard of performance than their experiences and physical maturity would allow.   In most cases it was found that pupils could learn

readily all the basic movements needed to use the machine for writing: insertion of paper, light striking of keys, spacing between words,
spacing between lines, complete return of the carriage, and use of the
shift key. The children who were more mechanically inclined
learned to operate such additional devices as back spacer, ribbon
reverse, and paper holders. In the systematic exercises which were
followed the use of two hands was started early. Most of the children in their informal writing used both hands for at least a part of
their work. Although these first grade children learned by observing that a skilled typist uses all her fingers and that certain keys are
struck by certain fingers, the use of all the fingers was not stressed.
Most of the children used one or two fingers; a few used as many as
three fingers at times. It did not seem justifiable to try to secure a
higher standard of performance in this respect.

Maintenance of a Feeling of Satisfaction by Control Pupils. Since each
class had to be divided into Control and Experimental divisions,
the children not using the typewriters were in the same room with
those using them. Accordingly, it was apparent that an unhappy
situation for Control pupils might be created.

At the beginning it was therefore explained to the Control children
that there were not enough machines for everyone and that they
would have a chance to use the machines at a later date. Some of
them were told that an effort was being made to find out how best
to use the typewriter in the first grade and that until it was found
out, certain chosen ones would use the machines. Then the others
could have their turn at using the typewriters. This promise
relieved a great many children to the extent that they expressed
no further desire to use the machines until the experiment ended;
and they were then happy to find that the promise was kept.

Especially during the first part of the experiment teachers made
efforts to direct the Control children in highly interesting activities
while the Experimental group was typing. It was quite common
to hear children say, "I am glad I am not typing. I would rather
be doing this."

It seemed that the teachers who had the least fear of unhappiness
arising had the least cause for anxiety. They took the matter-of-
course attitude with their pupils that, in words of more common
parlance, "we cannot always have what the Joneses have"; they
believed that this situation presented an ideal opportunity for learning that principle. Suggestions were offered to teachers and princi-

pals of schools; but they individually worked out a way for keeping Control groups satisfied.

The element of unhappiness did not enter in to any noticeable or appreciable extent.   It was found that this situation was not as difficult to control as had been anticipated.

Reading Instruction.   Effort was not exercised to change or standardize the methods of teaching reading by the different teachers. Each teacher proceeded as if no experiment were in progress.

City I.   It has already been pointed out how School A differed from the other schools in size of classes, intelligence of children, social environment, and amount of foreign language influence.   These factors largely determined a pronounced difference in the methods of teaching reading.   There were no prescribed teaching instructions in this school, and procedures were left entirely to the discretion of each teacher.

The following objectives seemed to be guiding the instruction of reading: (1) to develop strong motives for, and permanent interest in, reading; (2) to extend experience; (3) to stimulate thought; (4) to improve reading tastes; (5) to develop skill in the several different types of ability required in both the silent and the oral reading of work type and recreatory materials.

During the beginning stages no particular set of readers was used, but reading was taught largely as it entered into, or grew out of, children's activities and interests.   Activities involved were: (1) excursions or experiences (social, scientific, industrial, creative) with reading as an outgrowth; (2) composing charts, booklets, newspapers, etc.; (3) some practice in various reading books to develop skill; (4) some incidental drill in word recognition and phonics; (5) reading literature in connection with creative work, and also for aesthetic pleasure.

The unit of approach was a small but entire unit of thought, later analyzed into sentences, phrases, and words.   An approach was made through a variety of reading activities growing out of the children's whole school life, with major emphasis upon chart stories based on the children's own experiences and composed by them.

Later, systematized sets of readers were used along with numerous small books which could be selected from the library table.   Children read individually and in groups; they read silently and orally. Special skills, which were not developed in natural learning, were established through intrinsic devices; workbook reading materials, constructed for this purpose, were in use. Some incidental reference was made to phonetics in general lessons. The books used were mainly those published since 1930.

One teacher of the three in this school had a less mature class than did the others; the teaching of reading in this class was more incidental, comparatively speaking, and the beginning reading of the experiential type was done during the first half of the year. The experience reading was summed up in booklets with titles like "Charlie's Adventures," "My Visit to the Fire House." The children learned to know the direction of reading, to recognize vocabulary, to look at words critcally to note likenesses and differences, and to use the initial letters of words as aids to recognition. After Christmas they read from books. In groups they read: *Kit and Kat*, the *La Rue Book*, the Gates *Primer and First Reader*, the Elson-Gray *Primer and First Reader*, and the Gates *Peter and Peggy* workbook. Booklets and preprimers were used for home reading. Most of the children learned to read normally; the others received individual teaching of a nature to alleviate their specific difficulties.

City II. In City II the teachers followed, as a guide, the course of study made in 1925 by Isobel Davidson,[10] supervisor of elementary schools in this city.

An examination of this course of study shows that the general objectives are much like those which guided the instruction of the teachers in City I. The specific objectives are a listing of detailed habits of reading to be developed.

The statement is made that a library of simple, interesting, and well-illustrated material should be provided in every classroom. Suggestive lists of reading materials include picture books, nursery rhymes, alphabet books, scrapbooks, primers, first readers, story books, health booklets, and daily written messages. One primer and one first reader are to be used as basal texts for the class; others are supplementary. The basal readers listed make general provision for correlation with other subjects. The preprimer work is to be related closely to the children's needs and interests, through the use of incidental reading, silent reading and doing, and reading units. Emphasis is placed on the selection of content which will appeal to children's interests and lend itself to different types of silent reading exercises. The predominating subject matter contains realistic stories, informational selections, and silent reading

[10] Davidson, *op. cit.*

exercises in the form of narrative and expository materials and poems.

The activities engaged in are practice in exercises to increase comprehension and speed in silent reading, phrase and word drill including phonetic drill, and seat work calling for illustration of thoughts gained through reading.   Silent reading is always to precede oral reading.   The method of approach is usually reading directions silently and responding with dramatizations, drawings, or construction work; and the unit of approach is largely sentences or combinations of sentences.   The order of procedure is to develop sentences, phrases, words, and their meanings, and then lead children to note parts of words.   Drill is to be given on words in context, and it should follow the reading.   Some incidental reference is made to phonics in general lessons; but groups of individuals in need of phonetic practice are given special exercises.

Through observation of classroom instruction the director of the experiment concluded that the course of study was followed in general by all teachers.   An examination of each teacher's interpretation of her methods of teaching reading leads to the same conclusion. However, there was a marked tendency to use the latest reading materials rather than those listed in the outline, to integrate reading with everyday activities and units of work, to use intrinsic devices for developing the several important special skills not properly developed in ordinary natural learning, and to provide for individual differences among pupils.

Supervision of the Experiment.   The purposes of the supervision were: (1) to aid teachers in carrying out the plans formulated for a scientific investigation, (2) to observe in each classroom so that all existing conditions related to the study could be understood in terms of relationship to results obtained.

The supervision was done by the director of the experiment.   She was in constant contact with the classrooms of City I.   The schools in City II were visited usually every week—sometimes every two weeks.

Although written directions were sent to teachers whenever definitely defined procedures were to be followed, it is very evident that this kind of direction alone would not have been adequate. Individual conferences were held often with teachers to aid them to see the purposes of the study, its inherent organization of procedures, and how to deal with problems and complications which arose; the purpose of the conferences was also to help teachers evaluate past procedures and decide upon future plans, to better the type-writing instruction, to answer questions raised by the teachers, and to avoid letting the experiment interfere with the best possible de-velopment of pupils, schools, and communities.

Sometimes—especially during the early stages of typewriting instruction—actual demonstration was needed to show teachers how to proceed with typewriting teaching. In School A all the type-writing teaching was done by the director of the experiment.

Constant observation of classroom activities was made in order that the total situation could be understood, that no detrimental factors would be allowed to destroy the controllable features of the experiment, and that the progress of individual children might be followed.

Practically all the testing was done by the director of the experi-ment. The rest was done by individuals who were trained in the administration of scientific tests and in the teaching of primary children.

CHAPTER V

INTERPRETATION OF RESULTS

EQUALITY OF TYPEWRITER AND CONTROL GROUPS

THE preceding chapter shows how there was established an approximate equality of the Experimental and Control groups in all respects significant for learning reading save that the Experimental group had the use of the typewriters. It is the purpose of this chapter to summarize and chart the data collected.

That the Control and Typewriter groups were practically identical in mental age is shown in Table 5. The mean age in months for the Control group on October 1 was 77.20, with a standard deviation of 10.98. The mean for the Typewriter group was 77.19 months, with a standard deviation of 10.80. The difference between the means of .01 months is held to be insignificant for the purposes of the experiment.[1]

TABLE 5

Mean Mental Age in Months for Control and Typewriter Groups—October 1, 1931

Group	Number of Pupils	Mean Age in Months	S. D.	Difference between Means	S. D.$_{diff.}$	Difference S. D.$_{diff.}$
Control..........	113	77.20	10.98			
Typewriter.......	113	77.19	10.80	.01	1.45	.01

With respect to chronological age, the two groups were practically equivalent, as is shown in Table 6. The mean age in months for the Control group on October 1 was 74.81, with a standard deviation of 5.13; while the mean for the Typewriter group was 75.34 months, with a standard deviation of 4.75. The difference of .52 in months was small but in favor of the Typewriter group.

[1] For a discussion of the reliability of measures, see Garrett, Henry E., *Statistics in Psychology and Education*, Chap. III.

TABLE 6

Mean Chronological Age in Months for Control and Typewriter Groups—October 1, 1931

Group	Number of Pupils	Mean Age in Months	S. D.	Difference between Means	S. D.diff.	Difference / S. D.diff.
Control.........	113	74.81	5.13	.52	.66	.79
Typewriter.......	113	75.34	4.75			

Table 7 shows that in general intelligence the Control and Experimental groups were practically equal. The range of I. Q.'s for the Control group was 72–141, with the mean at 103.78 and the standard deviation 15.83. In the Experimental group the range was 71–146, with the mean at 102.86 and the standard deviation 16.06. The small difference of .92 in I. Q. favored the Control group.

TABLE 7

Intelligence Quotients of Control and Typewriter Groups as Measured by Detroit First Grade Intelligence and Stanford-Binet Tests

Group	Number of Pupils	Mean I. Q.	S. D.	Difference between Means	S. D.diff.	Difference / S. D.diff.
Control.........	113	103.78	15.83	.92	2.12	.43
Typewriter.......	113	102.86	16.06			

The total days of attendance at school by the Control group during the experimental period was 12,576, while the number of days of attendance by the Experimental group was 12,682. There is a total difference of 106 days in favor of the Experimental group; that is, on the average, each Experimental child attended school about one day more during the experiment than did each Control child. This fact should be taken into account in interpreting the differences between the two groups in the final tests.

The foregoing data indicate that at the beginning of the experiment the two groups were practically equivalent with respect to mental and chronological ages, and in intelligence scores; and that they were close to equality in number of days of school attendance.

GENERAL TRENDS IN TEST RESULTS

The purpose of this section is to compare the reading characteristics of the Experimental and Control groups.   The data showing results of the Experimental and Control groups on standardized tests are presented first.

Table 8 contains the records of all the children taking the tests in the different surveys.   As a result of the final equating, there were

TABLE 8

Mean Scores for Total Typewriter and Control Groups on All Tests Administered in January and in May, 1932

Test	Group	JANUARY					MAY				
		No. of Cases	Mean	S. D.	Diff. of Means	Diff. S. D.$_{\text{diff.}}$	No. of Cases	Mean	S. D.	Diff. of Means	Diff. S. D.$_{\text{diff.}}$
Gates Type 1*...........	X	98	3.28	4.92	1.46	2.62	106	15.98	11.53	2.91	1.63
	C	98	1.82	2.48			106	13.07	12.15		
Gates Type 2............	X	84	2.94	3.34	.61	1.28	100	11.83	9.10	1.42	1.13
	C	84	2.33	2.80			100	10.41	8.63		
Gates Type 3............	X	83	4.05	3.12	.09	.18	101	10.16	6.52	1.34	1.53
	C	83	3.96	2.94			101	8.82	5.92		
Detroit Word...........	X	82	6.11	5.66	.27	.31	95	17.72	8.91	1.16	.86
	C	82	5.84	5.50			95	16.56	9.67		
Haggerty Test 1..........	X	86	1.10	1.66	.20	.89	96	4.50	4.47	.49	.75
	C	86	.90	1.39			96	4.01	4.50		
Haggerty Test 2..........	X	86	.73	1.15	.25	1.56	96	2.31	2.70	.19	.46
	C	86	.48	1.00			96	2.12	2.90		
Gates Visual Perception A1	X	91	6.56	6.15	2.07	2.01					
	C	91	4.49	5.40							
Gates Visual Perception A3	X	79	11.05	6.73	3.15	2.60	97	19.69	8.70	2.57	1.93
	C	79	7.90	7.16			97	17.12	9.48		
Gates Visual Perception B2	X						104	8.90	4.86	1.27	1.93
	C						104	7.63	4.67		
Gray's Oral Score.........	X						88	1.06	.89	.21	1.57
	C						88	.85	.90		
Gray's Oral Speed.........	X						88	66.09	44.72	11.82	1.87
	C						88	54.27	39.11		

* Test administered in December, 1931 and May, 1932.

113 pupils in each group. However, fewer cases were considered in each of the test results owing to absences when tests were given; to maintain the equivalence of the total groups, each of a matched pair of subjects was excluded when one of them was absent. A summary of the test results in Table 8 indicates a constant tendency in reading growth favoring the Experimental pupils in all respects. This tendency to excel is impressive even though the differences between means on many of the tests were of little importance when considered alone.

Table 9 contains the records of one smaller group on three detailed individual tests given at two different times. In the data presented

TABLE 9

Mean Scores for Typewriter and Control Groups in City I on Gates Phonetic Ability Tests, Gates Pronunciation Test, and Gray's Reading Paragraphs — January and May, 1932

Test	Group	JANUARY					MAY				
		No. of Cases	Mean	S. D.	Diff. of Means	Diff. / S. D.diff.	No. of Cases	Mean	S. D.	Diff. of Means	Diff. / S. D.diff.
Gates Test of Phonetic Abilities											
A1	X	16	28.13*	6.59	−7.25	−2.29	13	20.23*	5.28	− 5.69	−1.75
	C	16	35.38	10.83			13	25.92	10.48		
A2	X	16	38.69†	14.53	−5.12	− .82	13	21.15†	6.27	−12.85	−2.36
	C	16	43.81	20.16			13	34.00	18.58		
A3	X	16	10.44	5.04	+1.37	+ .75	13	15.31	3.72	+ 3.62	+1.92
	C	16	11.81	5.39			13	11.69	5.74		
A4	X	16	7.31	7.62	+1.56	+ .52	13	14.23	11.60	+ 6.92	+1.42
	C	16	5.75	9.21			13	7.31	11.62		
A5	X	16	.22	.50	+ .03	+ .15	13	1.81	2.15	+ .77	+ .84
	C	16	.19	.73			13	1.04	2.17		
Gates Pronunciation	X	16	11.13	7.14	+2.19	+ .72	13	27.62	11.99	+ 5.39	+ .80
	C	16	8.94	9.91			13	22.23	21.05		
Gray's Oral Score	X	16	.26	.55	+ .05	+ .07					
	C	16	.21	.55							
Gray's Oral Speed	X	16	29.94	12.37	+2.94	+ .49					
	C	16	27.00	21.25							

* Number of seconds required to read capital letters.
† Number of seconds required to read lower case letters.

in Table 9 the reliability of differences was calculated. However, even an extremely large difference would be unreliable statistically since the number of cases is so small. In other words, there is little justification for using reliability measures in these small groups; but it is of value to notice the tendency of superiority of one group over another and to compare the consistency of these results with those of the total population.

Charts 1 and 2 aid in the interpretation of data from tests administered both in December or January and in May and recorded in Table 8; Chart 1 shows graphically the difference between mean scores of Experimental and Control groups on each of the tests and Chart 2 shows graphically how important these differences are. The obtained differences between the means of the two groups, although not outstandingly large in any instance, were found to be sufficiently large in most cases to insure considerably more than an even chance that the Experimental group would exceed the Control group on a retest. The most outstanding differences were found in Gates, Test 1 (word recognition) given in December and Gates, Visual Perception A3 (words) given in January. Closely following these were: Gates, Visual Perception A1 (objects), January; Gates, Visual Perception A3 (words), May; Gates, Visual Perception B2 (letters and words), and Gray's Oral (speed), May. Other differences between groups were found on the following tests listed in an order to correspond to the descending value or importance of the differences between means: Gates, Test 1 (word recognition), May; Haggerty, Test 2 (sentence reading), January; Gates, Test 3 (paragraph reading), May; Gray's Oral (score); Gates, Test 2 (word, phrase, and sentence reading), January; Gates, Test 2 (word, phrase, and sentence reading), May; Haggerty, Test 1 (paragraph reading), January; Detroit Word Recognition, May; Haggerty, Test 1, May; Haggerty, Test 2, May; and Detroit Word Recognition, January. The smallest difference between means of the Experimental and Control groups was found on the Gates, Test 3 (paragraph reading) given in January.

Although the differences between means in all test results favored the Experimental group, the value of those differences on May tests was greater sometimes and in some instances was less than on the December or January tests. From December or January to May the importance of the differences of means between groups increased noticeably in the following tests: Gates, Type 3 and Detroit Word

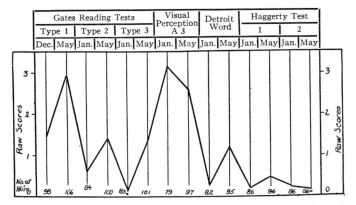

CHART 1. Difference between the Means of Typewriter and Control Groups on Each Test

The obtained difference between means was found by subtracting the mean of the Control group from the mean of the Typewriter group, since the latter had the highest average in each test.

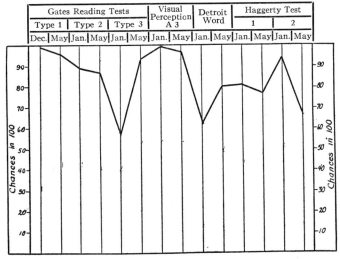

CHART 2. Reliability of Differences between Means of Typewriter and Control Groups, as Measured by Tests

This chart shows, on each test, the chances in one hundred that the true difference between Typewriter and Control pupils is greater than zero and in favor of the Experimental group.

Recognition Test. It diminished slightly in these tests: Gates, Type 1; Gates, Type 2; Gates, Visual Perception A3; Haggerty, Test 1. The importance of differences between means lessened considerably in Haggerty, Test 2 (see Chart 2).

The analysis of the data thus far shows that the differences in means favored the Experimental group always. The differences were most noteworthy in Gates Word Recognition Test administered in December and in the different Visual Perception Tests given in both January and May. Greatest increases in value of differences from January to May were found in Gates, Type 3 and in the Detroit Word Recognition Test; the test on which importance of differences diminished to an appreciable extent was Haggerty, Test 2.

ANALYSIS OF THE EXPERIMENTAL PROBLEM

The examination of data thus far points to general trends in results of tests given to all pupils. These data, along with other test results and evidences, are now interpreted with a view to supplying answers to the subordinate questions inherent in the definition of the major problem found on page 28.

Question 1. Do first grade children learn to read for thought more readily if typewriting is done? A summary of the data from this experiment indicates a tendency toward a positive answer to this question.

This question may be subdivided into three divisions.

The first sub-question deals with ability to read and comprehend complete paragraphs. The two tests which give major consideration to the answer are Gates, Type 3, and Haggerty, Test 1. On Gray's Oral Reading Paragraphs the comprehension was noted and teachers' judgments in this trait were also considered. Table 10 contains a summary of the data from the first two tests mentioned. Although the differences between the means in both January tests are very small and unimportant, the differences are in favor of the Experimental group. The same statement may be made concerning the May test results except that the difference between means on Gates, Type 3 is decidedly more outstanding. In Table 14 (page 74), showing an analysis of reading characteristics found by combining data derived from the teachers' judgments and Gray's Oral Paragraphs for all children, it will be noted that 11 children in the Experimental group and 21 children in the Control group were found to be outstandingly weak in reading comprehension. (Sixty-

TABLE 10

Mean Scores for Typewriter and Control Groups—Gates Primary Reading Test:
Reading of Directions; and Haggerty Reading Examination:
Sigma 1, Test 1—January and May, 1932

Test	Group	JANUARY					MAY				
		No. of Cases	Mean	S. D.	Diff. of Means	Diff. S. D.diff.	No. of Cases	Mean	S. D.	Diff. of Means	Diff. S. D.diff.
Gates Type 3............	X	83	4.05	3.12	.09	.18	101	10.16	6.52	1.34	1.53
	C	83	3.96	2.94			101	8.82	5.92		
Haggerty Test 1	X	86	1.10	1.66	.20	.89	96	4.50	4.47	.49	.75
	C	86	.90	1.39			96	4.01	4.50		

six pupils in the Experimental group and fifty-nine in the Control group were mentioned as outstanding cases of good comprehension.) From all the data considered, there is a constant tendency on the part of the Typewriter group to lead the Control group in ability to read and comprehend complete paragraphs.

The second sub-question deals with the effect of the typewriter on word, phrase, and sentence reading: ability to read verbal units of increasing complexity. In attempting to answer this question, analysis of data on Gates, Type 2 and on Haggerty, Test 2 are considered in Table 11. It is shown that the differences between groups were somewhat greater in January than in May.

TABLE 11

Mean Scores for Typewriter and Control Groups—Gates Primary Reading Test:
Word, Phrase, and Sentence Reading; and Haggerty Reading
Examination: Sigma 1, Test 2—January and May, 1932

Test	Group	JANUARY					MAY				
		No. of Cases	Mean	S. D.	Diff. of Means	Diff. S. D.diff.	No. of Cases	Mean	S. D.	Diff. of Means	Diff. S. D.diff.
Gates Type 2	X	84	2.94	3.34	.61	1.28	100	11.83	9.10	1.42	1.13
	C	84	2.33	2.80			100	10.41	8.63		
Haggerty Test 2	X	86	.73	1.15	.26	1.56	96	2.31	2.70	.19	.46
	C	86	.48	1.00			96	2.12	2.90		

There are very small differences between groups as registered by all of these tests; however, the very slight differences found favor the Experimental pupils.

The third sub-question is regarding the effect of typewriting on word recognition: ability to read words representative of the primary vocabulary. An analysis of data given in Table 12 shows this effect. Gates, Type 1 and the Detroit Word Recognition Test were used to find the results.

TABLE 12

Mean Scores for Typewriter and Control Groups—Gates Primary Reading Test: Word Recognition; and Detroit Word Recognition Test—January and May, 1932

Test	Group	JANUARY					MAY				
		No. of Cases	Mean	S. D.	Diff. of Means	$\frac{\text{Diff.}}{\text{S. D.diff.}}$	No. of Cases	Mean	S. D.	Diff. of Means	$\frac{\text{Diff.}}{\text{S. D.diff.}}$
Gates Type 1.............	X	98	3.28	4.92	1.46	2.62	106	15.98	11.53	2.92	1.63
	C	98	1.82	2.48			106	13.07	12.15		
Detroit Word............	X	82	6.11	5.67	.27	.31	95	17.72	8.91	1.16	.86
	C	82	5.84	5.50			95	16.56	9.67		

The most impressive difference here is found on Gates, Type 1, given in December. The reliability of difference of means on the same test given in May is slightly lower. On the Detroit Word Test given each time the reliability of differences is quite low, the standard difference being .31 for January and the slightly higher standard difference of .86 being for May. Here again, on all tests the differences in means always favored the Experimental group. Also, while the differences of means increased from January to May, the reliability of these differences decreased.

On every item denoting ability to read for thought and on every item for which a measurable instrument could be used, it was found that the Experimental group was slightly superior to the Control group.

Question 2. Is the typewriter used by first grade children conducive to their learning to read orally? Does it affect the oral reading process, phonetic and other analytic skills in the actual process of reading? Gray's Oral Reading Paragraphs were administered in January to the smaller group and in May to 176 pupils of the

total population to aid in answering this question.   Table 13 shows
the results of this survey.

TABLE 13

*Mean Scores for Typewriter and Control Groups—Gray's Oral Reading Paragraphs
Administered to Small Groups in January and to Larger Groups in May, 1932*

| Test | Group | JANUARY | | | | | MAY | | | | |
		No. of Cases	Mean	S. D.	Diff. of Means	Diff. S. D.diff.	No. of Cases	Mean	S. D.	Diff. of Means	Diff. S. D.diff.
Gray's Oral Score.........	X	17	.26	.55	.06	.07	88	1.06	.89	.21	1.57
	C	17	.21	.55			88	.85	.90		
Gray's Oral Speed........	X	17	29.90	12.37	2.90	.49	88	66.09	44.72	11.82	1.87
	C	17	27.00	21.25			88	54.27	39.10		

On the January test there is very little difference favoring the Experimental group.   On the May test, given to many more children, the
differences favoring Experimental pupils were much larger in abso-
lute value.   The greatest difference noted was in rapidity of reading: the Experimental children on the average read nearly 12 words
per minute more than did the Control pupils.

The analysis of reading characteristics in Table 14 shows the number of children in each total group who registered outstandingly in
any one of the traits listed.   For that reason just a few of the total
number of cases are listed for most of the traits, and the comparison
of these small numbers one against the other is of little importance.
However, it helps us to see what the trend or tendency is.

It will be seen that a few more of the children in the Experimental
group are rated as having a variety of attacks on word pronunciation
than in the Control group; 11 children in the Experimental group
seemed to have no method of attack at all while 27 in the Control
group were thought to have none.

Characteristics of good oral reading, such as grouping of words into
thought units, smoothness in reading, fluency, expression, and a
large eye span were next grouped together, and it was found that
there were 62 references to them in the Experimental group against
47 in the Control group.   At the same time there were 44 references
to wordy, jerky reading in the Experimental group with 55 references
to it in the Control group.

TABLE 14

Teachers' Judgments Concerning the Reading Characteristics of Pupils in the Typewriter and Control Groups *

	X	C
Attitude toward Reading		
Good	49	45
Average	19	19
Poor	24	25
Method of Attack		
Phonetic	22	22
Context	19	13
Configuration	13	9
Initial	11	9
Syllabication	5	4
Whole Word	1	2
Endings	1	1
Letter by letter	1	2
Combination of methods	14	5
No method	11	27
Characteristics of Reading Process		
Habit of grouping words in thought units resulting in smoothness, good expression, fluency, a good eye span	62	47
Wordy, jerky reading	44	55
Good comprehension	66	59
Poor comprehension	11	21
A non-reader	7	11
Habit of pointing to words	11	10
Some Determiners of Learning to Read		
Large vocabulary	27	19
No vocabulary	6	13
Good power of concentration	35	22
Little ability to concentrate	10	17
Good effort	11	10
Good home influence	35	30
Good social adjustment	19	13
Poor social adjustment	7	8
Timidity	17	6
Poor eyesight	4	8
Poor health	12	4
Immaturity	7	7
Foreign language influence	6	7
Lack of readiness	6	13

* This table shows the number of children in each total group who were thought to possess the reading traits listed. The teachers' judgments were supplemented by remarks made on the Gray's Oral Test administered in May.

There were evidences of better comprehension in the Experimental group from which 77 cases were reported and compared with 80 cases in the Control group.

More references were made to handicaps and inabilities, especially inability to concentrate and small vocabulary, in the Control group than in the Experimental group.

The first grade children who used typewriters tended to be superior in oral reading ability, even though the differences in most of the individual traits were small and insignificant when considered alone.

Question 3. Do first grade children who use typewriters have better methods of studying and recognizing words? Are their word pronunciation and methods of attacking words more effective? How does the use of the typewriter affect ability to recognize and deal in certain ways with individual word elements? Insofar as the data in Table 9 are reliable, they indicate that in City I the Experimental pupils could pronounce words in isolation on Gates Pronunciation Test just a little better than the Control pupils. The average difference between groups amounted to only two words, with a standard difference of .72.

The results of the Gates Phonetic Abilities Tests given to 16 selected children in each group are used as suggestive evidences of effects on ability to recognize and deal in certain ways with individual word elements. The mean scores for Test A1 are in terms of numbers of seconds needed to read the capital letters. In January the Control pupils on the average needed 7.25 seconds more, with a standard difference of 2.29; in May the Control pupils on the average needed 5.69 seconds more, with a standard difference of 1.75. On Test A2 given in January it took the Control children 5.12 seconds longer to read the lower case letters, with a standard difference of only .82; in May this difference favoring Experimental pupils rose to 12.85 seconds, with a standard difference of 2.36.

Test A3 measured ability to give sounds of letters in terms of numbers of letters correctly translated into sounds. In January the Control pupils on the average could sound 1.37 letters more, with a standard difference of .75; while in January the Experimental pupils on the average could sound 3.62 letters more, with a standard difference of 1.92.

The ability to translate printed phonograms into sounds was measured by Test A4. In January Experimental pupils had an excess average of 1.56 phonograms, with a standard difference of

.52; in May the Experimental excess average was 6.92 phonograms, with a standard difference of 1.42.

Very little difference between groups either in January or in May was found in ability to give sounds of combinations of phonograms as measured by Test A5. The differences favoring Experimental pupils were .03, with a standard difference of .15 in January, and .77, with a standard difference of .84 in May.

It will be seen that the January differences were very slight, with the exception of those in ability to read capital letters. In May the distinctions between groups became more pronounced in all respects except in ability to read capital letters. The Experimental group was superior in every item except A3 for January.

Question 4. Do first grade children who use typewriters register greater speed in reading? On the Gray's Oral Reading Test given in May (see Table 8, page 66) an outstanding difference of an average of twelve words more per minute was in favor of the Experimental group. The same test administered to the smaller group in January revealed an average difference of three words per minute favoring the Experimental group. A summary of these data indicate a tendency toward a positive answer to this question.

Question 5. How does the use of the typewriter by first grade children affect their visual perception? Gates, Visual Perception Test, A1 was used as an instrument to measure visual perception of geometrical designs. This test was given in January only (see Table 8, page 66). The difference of means in terms of raw score was 2.07 with a standard difference of 2.01. As it is, the chances are about 98 in 100 [2] that the average score of the Experimental pupils would be higher than the average score of the Control group on a retest.

Gates, Visual Perception Test, A3, to measure perception of words, was administered in January and in May. The means of raw scores of each group were found and the difference between these means in January was 3.15. The obtained difference, with a standard difference of 2.60, is large enough to guarantee that almost always the average score of the Experimental pupils will be higher than the average score of the Control pupils. On the May test the difference between means was 2.57 and the standard difference of 1.93 indicates that 97 times in 100 [2] the average score of the Experimental group will be higher than the average score of the Control pupils.

[2] Garrett, *op. cit.*, p. 134.

Gates, Visual Perception Test, B2, perceiving words and selecting one among many for matching, was given in May only. Here the obtained difference is only 1.27 with a standard difference of 1.93.

Although none of the obtained differences between means on Visual Perception Tests is large enough to guarantee a completely reliable difference between means, all are large enough to indicate that the average scores of the Experimental children on a retest will be higher than those of the Control children. The most outstanding difference was found in perception of words in January.

Question 6. How does the use of the typewriter by first grade children affect their interest in reading? It is difficult to measure interest in reading; but two items which could be defined were chosen as evidences. It seemed that the correlation between interest in reading and amount of reading done by an individual should be high; also, if a child chose to read in preference to doing anything else during a free activity period, it seemed that this showed evidence of a reading interest. The names of books read by each child throughout the year were therefore listed by teachers.

First, regardless of the size or nature of the reading material, the number of books read by each child was found. The mean number read by each group was computed and it was found that the difference between these means in favor of the Experimental group was only .57 of a book.

An examination of the books read by 196 pupils paired into Experimental and Control groups indicates the character of the reading done. Table 15 shows that 450 primers were read by Experimental pupils and 414 primers were read by Control pupils; 220 first readers were read by Experimental children and 195 first readers by Control children; six second readers were read by Experimental pupils while

TABLE 15

Number of Primers, First Readers, Second Readers, and Supplementary Books Read by Children in Typewriter and Control Groups during the Experimental Period

Group	Number of			
	Primers	First Readers	Second Readers	Supplementary Books
Control..........	414	195	2	111
Typewriter........	450	220	6	102

two second readers were read by Control pupils; and among the library books listed 102 of them were read by the Experimental group and 111 by the Control group. It was found that the kind of reading was quite the same for each group; in general, each book listed was read by approximately the same number of pupils from each group. These data may indicate that typewriting has little or no effect upon the choice of reading materials.

It will be recalled that in January and in May each teacher provided for a "free period" of thirty minutes during which each child was allowed to choose whatever he desired to do. The names of children who chose reading as an activity were recorded. Table 16 shows little difference between groups, but the difference favors pupils who used typewriters.

TABLE 16

Number of Children Choosing to Read During Free Activity Periods

Amount of Reading	JANUARY		MAY	
	X	C	X	C
Read during entire period...	50	41	23	11
Read during part of period..	9	15	9	9
Did no reading............	52	55	44	56
Total number of children..	111	111	76	76

On the basis of the two evidences of interest which were noted, it may be concluded that there was little difference between the two groups, but that this difference was in favor of the pupils who used typewriters.

Question 7. How does typewriting by first grade pupils affect their general reading and detailed characteristics of their reading according to the rating by classroom teachers?

The teachers were asked to pass judgment on the reading abilities of each of their pupils in accordance with directions found on pages 41–42. The ratings in terms of A, B, C, D, and E were translated into numerical figures thus: A = 90–99; B = 80–89; C = 70–79; D = 60–69; E = 50–59. In January the Experimental group had slightly higher ratings on the average; the difference in means was 2.41. In May the small difference between means of 2.99 again favored the Experimental pupils. The small differences between groups in the January and May ratings hold practically the same statistical value.

Table 14 (page 74) shows comparison of groups on detailed characteristics of reading. Comparisons on individual items should not be taken too seriously, because the numbers of subjects are too small. However, it shows tendencies of superiority of the Experimental children in good and varied attacks on word pronunciation, in smooth and expressive reading against wordy or jerky reading, and in ability to comprehend. There are more handicaps and specific reading inabilities recorded against the Control pupils.

On the whole there is little difference between the two groups, but this small difference tends to favor pupils who used typewriters.

COMPARATIVE GAINS OF TYPEWRITER AND CONTROL GROUPS ON ALL TESTS ADMINISTERED TWICE

Since the several tests taken at two different times during the school year had to be matched for the same individuals, it was necessary for the number of cases to be less than that of the total group. Averages of the Experimental gains and the Control gains on the three Gates Primary Reading Tests, the Gates Visual Perception Test A3, the Detroit Word Recognition Test, and the Haggerty Reading Examination, Sigma 1 have been computed. Chart 3 presents the gains of the Experimental and Control pupils on each test separately. All gains are expressed in terms of raw scores, since some of the scores are too low and in others provision is not made for translating them into tenths of a grade. The gains were computed by subtracting the average December or January status from the average final status. The bars in Chart 3 represent these differences. The most important evidence found here is based upon the indications of the differences found on individual tests. If the gains on the three different Gates Reading Tests were translated into grade units, it would show an excess gain of one month on each test in favor of the Experimental children. The difference between gains on the other tests are very small. It is not feasible to calculate the average of the Experimental gains on all tests since these averages are unweighted. It is sufficient to conclude that the Experimental group made an excess gain of one month on each of the Gates Primary Tests from December or January to the end of May and a very small excess gain on the Visual Perception, Haggerty, and Detroit Word tests during the same period.

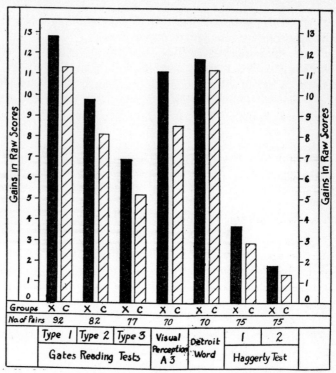

CHART 3.   Comparative Gains of Typewriter and Control Groups from
January to May, 1932, as Measured by Tests

The difference between the raw scores are here shown by the vertical bars in score
units.   The bars are arbitrarily set upon a straight base line for convenience of
reading.   The black bars represent gains of the Typewriter groups.

COMPARATIVE GAINS OF BRIGHT, NORMAL, AND DULL PUPILS

It is interesting to find whether the bright or normal or dull pupils
profited most in reading by the use of typewriters.   Some observers
have expressed the opinion that the bright pupils would be helped
most since their acquisition of skill in typing would probably be
greater.   Others have suggested that the typewriter would be most
adaptable to progress of dull children.   Actual observations in
classrooms have revealed evidences of real assistance to reading
development among all classes of children.   Most of the teachers
thought that the typewriter helped both the bright and the dull
pupils about equally.

The purpose of Chart 4 is to show the average gains in the reading tests given to the Experimental and Control children when they were divided into five intelligence quotient levels.

Our study of comparative gains on different intelligence levels must be based on fewer cases, since the several tests taken four or five months apart had to be matched for the same individuals and the intelligence quotient for each subject of a pair had to fall within the same intelligence range. This chart shows in raw scores the average

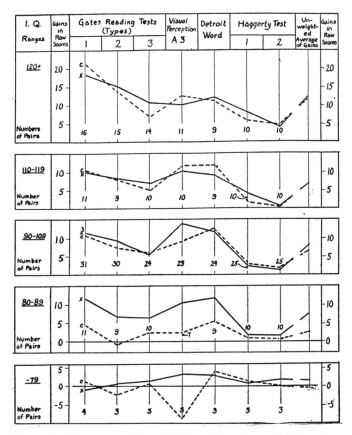

CHART 4. Comparative Gains of Bright, Normal, and Dull Pupils in Typewriter and Control Groups from January to May, 1932

The gains on indicated tests of the Typewriter and Control pupils in each intelligence quotient level are shown in terms of raw score units. The unweighted averages of the Typewriter and Control gains in each level are shown at the extreme right. The points representing Typewriter gains are connected by solid lines, those representing Control gains by dash lines.

gains, on tests administered in January and May, of the Experimental and Control children when they have been divided into five intelligence quotient levels. Taking an unweighted average of the Experimental gains and of the Control gains in the seven tests in each intelligence quotient group facilitates this comparison. These unweighted averages have been plotted on Chart 4 and show that the gain of the Experimental children is about equal to the Control gain in the two highest intelligence quotient groups. The difference favoring Experimental pupils becomes more pronounced on the 90–109 level. The greatest superiority of the Experimental group over the Control group is in the two lowest intelligence quotient levels. The pupils whose reading was helped most by the use of the typewriter were those in the 80–89 intelligence groupings. The use of unweighted averages prevents a comparison of gains on one test with another, but it does not notably vitiate the comparisons of excess gains of the various intelligence quotient groups.

The data for comparing gains of pupils on the different intelligence levels implies that the total excess gains in reading made by the Experimental group may be attributed to the progress of the pupils in the lower ranges of intelligence.

TEACHERS' OPINIONS CONCERNING THE EFFECT OF TYPEWRITING ON READING

The ten teachers in this experiment were asked to state their opinions of the effects of typewriting on beginning reading. Four of them expressed the opinion that the typewriter had a decidedly good effect. One teacher wrote, "The typewriting had a good effect on learning to read on all but one of the Experimental group. The children could express themselves better by the use of the typewriter. It was a new experience and they were so pleased when they had written something which they could read. Many could go to the typewriter and write a sentence without hesitation. It taught them to recognize the letters of the alphabet and to see the connection between the letters and reading. The one child who was not helped was unresponsive ordinarily; and although he typed fairly well, there was no effect on reading. It is just within the last three or four weeks of the school year that he has shown any reading ability at all." Another report expressed a belief in the positive effect of typing on reading because practically all the failures in reading were outside the Experimental group. The teacher stated,

"My opinion is based on a general feeling, without any particular evidence to substantiate it." The third teacher thought that the typewriter had a good influence on beginning reading because it developed an interest in accuracy and neatness, the children wanted to come to school and so the attendance was increased, it developed an interest in reading, and it aided word perception. This teacher reported, "This is the first grade I have had to show such a keen interest in spelling and a desire to make word lists." The fourth teacher who expressed the opinion that the typewriter had a good effect said, "The interest in reading became keener because of type-writing. The children learned to note differences in sounds and letters. They were eager to learn what certain words meant so that they could use them in typewriting original work. Their vocabularies were enlarged somewhat."

Five teachers could not find evidence to make them believe that the typewriters had decidedly good or decidedly bad effects on the reading of their Experimental pupils. Two of these teachers said that their pupils who were typing were reading better than the Control pupils but that they did not know whether the typewriter had caused the difference. One of these two said that she had never before had a class so interested in spelling and in accumulating word lists. Another teacher remarked, "I do not think that typewriting had any influence on learning to read during this first year. Now that the children know how to use typewriters, I feel sure that typewriting will have a decided effect during the second year."

Only one teacher expressed a divided opinion and listed a bad as well as a good influence. She wrote, "In three cases out of eight in the Experimental group, the children became symbol conscious. They used the letter instead of the phonetic method of attack on words. It seemed to affect the length of the eye span. One pupil enjoyed reading what he typed, thus giving him more experience in reading; other members of the group did not do this. In general, the children of both groups seemed equally interested in reading. One group was comparable to the other in reading progress; the same number from each group were on identical reading levels."

It will be seen from these remarks that most of the teachers saw no outstanding evidences of good or bad effects of typewriting on reading. Only one of the other teachers noted any harmful effects; four expressed the opinion that typewriting had a good influence on learning to read.

Variety and Quantity of Typewriting Done by Experimental Pupils

It is obvious that a knowledge of the quantity, variety, and quality of the typewritten materials produced by the Experimental children is important in judging the values of the new writing device.

In an examination of all the papers a wide variety of writings were found. On the average 355 practice exercises for the first grade constructed by Dr. Ralph Haefner were used by the different classes. Besides this, the writings consisted of:

Writing of names.
Writing of numbers and characters.
Writing of letters of the alphabet.
Writing of the date on paper.
Writing addresses.
Original writings.
   Poems.
   Birthday, Christmas, New Year, and Valentine greetings.
   Notices for bulletin board.
   Words which could be spelled.
   Letters and invitations to friends, parents, the principal, Santa Claus, and
      others.
   News items for the class newspaper.
   Riddles.
   Original sentences.
   Names of people the children knew.
   Compositions about classroom activities and outside experiences.
   Writing descriptions of pets, the circus, and other interesting things.
   Lists of words that rhyme.
   Stories which were reproduced.
   Stories and titles of pictures for a booklet.
Copied writings.
   Names of people.
   Selections from readers and other sources, including narration, description,
      directions, poems, plays, sentences, phrases, and words.
   Titles of stories and poems.
   Numbers.
   Days of the week.
   Programs.
   Answers to questions: Yes and No.
   Arithmetic work.
   Enumeration of things or objects belonging to one class.

An effort was made to find the average number of words written per pupil, also showing separately the average number of words of copied material, of original material, and of drill material for training in skill. The results of this study are based on the findings in the folder of an average pupil for each typewriting class. The term "average pupil" refers to the pupil whose writings indicated an average of his class in typewriting performance in terms of quality, quantity, and variety of materials produced. The writings of these selected pupils were sorted according to the above classification and the number of words written under each grouping was counted. The sum of the words in each classification was divided by the number of classrooms to find the average number of words for each pupil. The results show that on the average 4,410 words were written by each pupil. This included an average of 235 words of copied material, 451 words of original material, and 3,724 words of drill material for training in skill. The magnitude of the task of counting every word on every paper made it necessary to collect the data by the method described in this paragraph.

Typewriting Speed and Accuracy

The skill in the use of the typewriter which was acquired by the children of the Experimental group is significant in the light of results obtained in reading. Two characteristics of typing call for measurement; they are (1) rate and (2) quality. The rate is computed in terms of number of letter spaces written in one minute. The quality is computed in terms of index error; this is found by dividing the total number of errors by the total number of letter spaces written. The errors are here classified:

1. Punctuation and Spelling Errors.
   a. Capital letter in place of small letter.
   b. Small letters at beginning of sentence.
   c. Misspellings.
   d. Period omitted at end of sentence.
   e. Failure to indent.

2. Accuracy of Copying.
   a. One character written over another.
   b. Order of letters reversed.
   c. Substitution for word in test material.
   d. Insertion of character or group of characters.
   e. Wrong character used.

3. Operation of the Typewriter.
   a. Failure to space between words.
   b. Capital letter out of line.

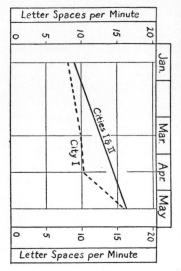

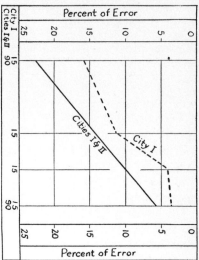

CHART 5.   Mean Typing Rates of Experimental Pupils Who Had Typing Rate Tests

The points representing rates of ninety pupils in Cities I and II combined are connected by solid lines; those pupils took typing rate tests both in January and in May.   The points representing rates of fifteen pupils in City I are connected by dash lines; those pupils took typing rate tests in January, March, April, and May.

CHART 6.   Mean Typing Error Index of Pupils Who Took Typing Rate Tests

In order to obtain an objective measure of the rate and quality of typing, two equivalent forms of tests for first grade, devised by Dr. Ralph Haefner, were used.   Of the 113 Experimental pupils, 3 did not take either the January or the May tests.   Twenty children took only one of the two tests, and so were not included.   The 90 children who took both the January and the May tests are included in Charts 5 and 6.   On the average these children wrote 8.91 letter spaces per minute in January after using the typewriters for three months, and 16.22 letter spaces per minute in May after using them for seven months.   In January the index error was 22.95 per cent, whereas in May it was 5.87 per cent.   To show the continuity of growth among 15 children in City I, the test was given four different times from January to May.   The greatest gain in rate was during the last month of the school year, while the greatest gain in accuracy was from March to April.   All the children who did typing made greater gains in accuracy than in speed, and gain in accuracy seemed to precede gain in speed.

READING AND WRITING BY CONTROL PUPILS DURING TYPEWRITING PERIODS

In the final interpretation of results it is necessary to take into consideration the amount of emphasis upon reading and writing by Control pupils during the time when Experimental pupils were typewriting. During the period of the investigation an average total of 2,400 minutes was spent on typewriting by each Experimental group. We are concerned with the reading and writing done by the Control group during this time when both groups were working as separate units.

The amount of emphasis upon reading by Control groups during this time can be determined only approximately. The first grade programs designated that an average of one-fifth of the school time be specifically set aside for reading instruction. Accordingly, about one-fifth of the twenty-four hundred minutes, or about four hundred and eighty minutes, was spent on learning to read by each Control group. This does not include the reading by Control pupils in connection with activities closely allied to reading; but the typewriting also, to some extent, was integrated with reading.

Only an estimate of the amount of writing done by Control pupils during the designated time could be determined, since it was impossible to secure a count of all words written by each child. An analysis of teachers' descriptions and children's papers indicates that an average of 105 words were written by each Control child; this is just about 2 per cent of the amount of writing done on the typewriter (see page 85).

It is important to take into account the additional amount of time spent on learning to read by Control pupils and the additional amount of emphasis upon verbal units by Experimental pupils in interpreting the differences between the two groups in the reading tests.

CHAPTER VI

SUMMARY AND CONCLUSIONS

Summary of Results

It has been shown how the need for this study arose. The history of writing and of the typewriter is a story of the slow development of a system and means of written communication so perfected today that it promises to be adaptable to meet the needs of the very young child. A history of development of methods of teaching reading shows why at this time, more than ever before, primary reading specialists and educators are concerned with the effects of typewriting on beginning reading. Previous experimentation has intensified the need for the present study by indicating that the typewriter, as an educational instrument, can be used in the kindergarten and the first grade.

This investigation has concerned itself with effects of typewriting on learning to read in the first grade. Typewriting has not been substituted, in this experiment, for any other system of writing; it has not been placed in the program of the first grade at the loss of any other one subject or activity. Each subject or activity of the curriculum has suffered a loss of equal importance to allow time for the introduction of typewriting.

It has been explained why the equivalent-groups method of experimentation was chosen. The method of equating pupils within classrooms was for the purpose of keeping constant the teacher influence and other factors inherent in determining the development of individual classes. On the basis of mental ages the Experimental and the Control groups were practically equivalent. It was found that on the average each Experimental child attended school about one day more during the school year than did each Control child. This factor of attendance was also taken into consideration in the final equating of subjects.

The customary precautions were taken in planning and carrying out the experiment to secure results that were statistically reliable. The aim was to use a sufficiently large number of subjects as a representative sampling but small enough to warrant a careful and detailed study of the problem. The experiment ran for seven uninterrupted school months which approached equivalence to a usual school year.

No effort was made toward standardizing the teaching of reading among teachers, but an effort was made to define the character of this teaching. Most of the teachers had sufficient skill in the use of typewriters, and steps were taken by the others to obtain the needed skill before the experiment started. Written instructions on typewriting teaching were in the hands of each teacher. In every instance a combined method of systematic and informal teaching was followed.

The Control group in this experiment proceeded in carrying on a normal first grade program; the Experimental group carried on the same program except that typewriting was done from 75 to 90 minutes per week, which necessitated that much less time on all other activities in their proper proportions.

The reading achievement of the total groups was measured by the following tests in December or January and in May: Gates Primary Reading Tests, Types 1, 2, and 3; Detroit Word Recognition; Haggerty Reading Examination, Sigma 1; and Gates Visual Perception A3. On all these tests the differences between means were quite small and not very important, and on some tests the difference was barely noticeable; but in every instance these differences favored the Experimental group. The greatest differences were found in word recognition and in the perception of words. Gates Visual Perception A1 was administered in January only to the total population and a difference of means in raw score of 2.07 favored the Experimental group with a standard difference of 2.01. The tests given to the total population in May only were: Gray's Oral Reading Paragraphs and Gates Visual Perception B2. In oral reading there was a difference between means of .21 of a grade with a standard difference of 1.57; the difference in rate was 11.82 words per minute with a standard difference of 1.87. Both differences favored the Experimental pupils. The difference on Visual Perception B2 favored the Typewriter group by 1.28 points in raw score with a standard difference of 1.93.

On individual tests administered to only sixteen selected children in each group to measure ability to pronounce words in isolation and to deal in certain ways with word elements it was found that in both January and May, with one exception, the Experimental pupils always led the Control pupils. In January the Experimental group showed the most marked superiority in ability to read the capital letters. In every other item measured the differences favoring Experimental pupils showed a marked increase in May over the January differences.

In answer to every detailed question listed in the analysis of the experimental problem it has been found that there is very little difference between the two groups, but the tendency for the Experimental group to excel is apparent.

In comparing the gains on tests taken in December or January and May and matched for the same individuals, it was found that the gains of the Experimental pupils were greater than the gains of the Control pupils on all tests. There was an even superiority of gain of one month on each of the Gates Primary Reading Tests. On Gates Visual Perception A3, Detroit Word, and Haggerty tests there was a small excess gain.

In comparing the gains of bright, normal, and dull children it was shown that the reading of pupils in the lower ranges of intelligence was helped most by the use of the typewriter. Since the gains of the two groups were equivalent in the upper ranges, the total excess gains by the Experimental group may be due to the progress of pupils having I. Q.'s below 90.

In an analysis of the actual reading of pupils on the Gray's Oral Reading Paragraphs and in the everyday reading of pupils noted by teachers, it seemed evident that the Experimental pupils read with more fluency, with better expression, and with smoothness—a fact which indicated the presence of a larger eye span; more instances of wordy, jerky reading were noted among Control pupils. These sources also revealed better comprehension on the part of Experimental pupils. The pupils who used typewriters seemed to have better attacks on word pronunciation and slightly fewer lacks in a fundamental background for learning to read.

Measures which could be used revealed an almost equal interest in reading by both groups.

Most of the teachers in this experiment saw no outstanding evidences of good or bad effects of typewriting on reading. Less than one-half of them were of the opinion that its effects were decidedly good. One teacher listed some bad effects along with good ones.

An analysis of materials typewritten by children in the Experimental group showed that on the average 4,410 words were written by each child during the year.   This included 3,724 words of drill material for training in skill, 451 words of original material, and 235 words of copied material.   Results of tests show that after using the typewriters for three months, on the average, these children wrote 8.91 letter spaces per minute, with 22.95 per cent error.   After using the typewriters for seven months, they could write, on an average, 16.22 letter spaces per minute, with only 5.87 per cent error.   Progress in accuracy seemed to precede progress in speed.

In accordance with the experimental set-up, the Control pupils spent approximately 480 minutes more during the investigation on learning to read than did the Experimental children.   An analysis of teachers' descriptions and children's papers indicated that on the average the Control child wrote by hand just about 2 per cent of the number of words written on the typewriter by the Experimental child during the periods when the two groups were working as separate units.

CONCLUSIONS

In the interpretation of results of this experiment certain limitations must necessarily be considered.   On no one item measured was there a large enough number of children to warrant a highly reliable statistical interpretation.   These interpretations were included as suggestive of general trends and not as conclusive evidence.

It should be kept in mind also that there were decided limitations in equating groups on the trait in question in this experiment. Although none of the children in either group showed any notable skill in reading at the beginning of the year, yet it is reasonable to suppose that some inherent and acquired powers were present which could not be measured accurately by an existing instrument.   An effort was made to eliminate this disadvantage by selecting intelligence tests adapted to measuring aptitude in reading and by administering them as skillfully as possible.

It should be remembered also that the children in the Experimental group had more experience with verbal units as an integral part of their typewriting.   This experience, apart from the typewriter, may have produced desirable effects on reading.   However, this possible advantage is balanced partly by the additional amount of time spent by the Control group on learning to read.

With these qualifications in mind, the following conclusions may be drawn:

1. That the results of all tests and of subjective evidence used to define achievements in beginning reading indicate a trend of slight but constant superiority on the part of pupils who used typewriters.

2. That the pupils who used typewriters showed the most outstanding superiority in the following reading abilities: to recognize words, to perceive words, to read rapidly and fluently, to deal in certain ways with word elements, and, by the end of the year, to gain comprehension.

3. That the gains in reading ability of pupils who used typewriters from December or January to May were more pronounced than the gains in reading ability of Control pupils.

4. That the children in the lower ranges of intelligence were the ones whose progress in reading was aided most by the use of typewriters. On the upper and middle ranges of intelligence there was not much difference between groups. These comparisons, however, were made on the basis of raw scores and unweighted averages and should therefore not be interpreted too broadly.

5. That teachers of individual groups of children tended slightly toward noticing a good effect of typewriting on beginning reading.

6. That the children who used typewriters did more writing than did children who relied upon pencils alone.

All these data indicate that the beginning reading of children who do typewriting is slightly superior in every noticeable respect to that of pupils who do not use typewriters.

It is possible that more pronounced differences between groups or an opposite tendency of results might be found if this experiment were to be repeated with a different kind of population or if a different method of teaching reading or typewriting were in use. However, if the second experiment were to concern itself with a detailed study of reading characteristics, the general trend of results would probably lead to the same direction of tendency found in this experiment.

IMPLICATIONS OF THE STUDY

The disadvantages and limitations of total reliance on handwriting as a means of written expression by the very young child have been observed frequently. Experimentation has revealed the fact that the typewriter does stimulate fluency in the original writing of first grade children without any apparent sacrifice in other forms of achievement. Instead of competing with handwriting productivity, the use of the typewriter has tended to increase handwriting output in the lower grades.

Previous experimentation along with this study presents strong evidence: (1) "that it is feasible to use the typewriter in the conduct of the ordinary work of the first grade; (2) that the teachers regard the typewriter as a valuable educational instrument and approve its use in their own classes, while the pupils enjoy typewriting and look upon the typewriter with marked favor." [1]

The important result of this study is not that typewriting promotes learning to read, but rather that typewriting, as carried on in this experiment, does not harm the reading of first grade pupils taught by the more progressive methods. If the real influence of typewriting on reading is as favorable as that indicated by the results of the present study, school administrators and primary teachers and supervisors who are concerned primarily with effective development of beginning reading should not hesitate to introduce typewriters as educational instruments in the kindergarten and primary grades.

[1] Wood and Freeman, *An Experimental Study of the Educational Influences of the Typewriter in the Elementary Grades*, p. 184.

BIBLIOGRAPHY

SELECTED REFERENCES

ALLTUCKER, M. M. "Teaching of Handwriting." *Journal of National Education Association*, XVI: 25–26, 1927.

BACHELER, A. W. "The Typewriter in the Public Schools." *Education*, XIX: 626–633, 1899.

COLLINS, JAMES H. "The Story of the Typewriter." *St. Nicholas*, XLXI: 486–495, 1922.

DOUGHERTY, M. L. "History of the Teaching of Handwriting in America." *Elementary School Journal*, XVIII: 280–286, 1917.

FOLLETT, MRS. HELEN THOMAS. "Education a la Carte." *Pictorial Review*, XXX: 2, 1929.

FOLLETT, MRS. HELEN THOMAS. "Education via the Typewriter." *Parents*, VII: 22–24, 1932.

FREEMAN, F. N. "Experiment in the Use of Typewriters in the Elementary School." *Elementary School Journal*, XXXII: 752–759, 1932.

GARRETT, HENRY E. *Statistics in Psychology and Education.* Longmans, Green & Company, New York, 1930.

GATES, A. I. *New Methods in Primary Reading.* Bureau of Publications, Teachers College, Columbia University, New York, 1928.

GATES, A. I. "Problems in Beginning Reading." *Teachers College Record*, XXVI: 572–591, 1925.

GATES, A. I. *The Improvement of Reading.* The Macmillan Company, New York, 1929.

GATES, A. I. "The Supplementary Device versus the Intrinsic Method of Teaching Reading." *Elementary School Journal*, XXV: 775–786, 1925.

HAEFNER, RALPH. *The Typewriter in the Primary and Intermediate Grades.* The Macmillan Company, New York, 1932.

KASSON, FRANK H. "The Typewriter a Coming Necessity in Schools." *Education*, XV: 615–623, 1895.

LIPMAN, MICHAEL. *A History of the Alphabet.* Royal Typewriter Company, Bureau of Research, 1930.

McCALL, WILLIAM A. *How to Experiment in Education.* The Macmillan Company, New York, 1926.

MOWRY, WILLIAM A. "The Educational Use of the Typewriter in Schools." *Education*, XI: 625–638, 1891.

PALMER, FRANK H. "Educational Aspects of Typewriting." *Education*, XII: 622–626, 1892.

REILEY, ALAN C. "The Typewriter—Now the Children Are Making It 'Click.'" *Junior Home*, 1933.

SMITH, NILA B. "An Historical Analysis of American Reading Instruction." Unpublished Doctor's dissertation, Columbia University, June, 1931.

STEDMAN, M. B. "Study of the Possibility of Prognosis of School Success."
Journal of Applied Psychology, XIII: 505–515, 1929.

TAYLOR, ISAAC. *The Alphabet.* Kegan Paul, Trench, and Company, London,
1883.

TERMAN, LEWIS M. *The Measurement of Intelligence.* Houghton Mifflin Company, Boston, 1916.

·WALDO, FRANK. "Educational Use of the Typewriter." *Education*, XII: 484–
492, 1902.

·WOOD, BEN D. "The Typewriter in the Grades. *Grade Teacher*, L: 350–353,
1933.

WOOD, BEN D. AND FREEMAN, FRANK N. *An Experimental Study of the Educational
Influences of the Typewriter in the Elementary Classroom.* The Macmillan Company,
New York, 1932.

ADDITIONAL REFERENCES

DAVIDSON, ISOBEL. *First Grade Reading Course of Study for Elizabeth, New Jersey,*
1925.

Encyclopedia Britannica: Alphabet, Vol. 1, pp. 677–684, 1929.

Palaeography, Vol. XVII, pp. 96–102, 1929.

Pictography, Vol. XVII, pp. 913–914, 1929.

The Story of the Typewriter. The Herkimer County Historical Society of Herkimer,
New York, 1923.

The Typewriter in Child Education. Typewriter Educational Research Bureau,
230 Park Avenue, New York, 1932.

Scientific American. "Some Milestones in the Development of the Typewriter."
129: 165, 1923.

Typewriter History and Encyclopedia. Business Equipment Publishing Company,
New York. Reprinted edition from October, 1923 issue of *Typewriter Tonics.*